jQuery Design Patterns

Learn the best practices on writing efficient
jQuery applications to maximize performance
in large-scale deployments

Thodoris Greasidis

BIRMINGHAM - MUMBAI

jQuery Design Patterns

First published: February 2016

Production reference: 1230216

Published by Packt Publishing Ltd.
Livery Place
35 Livery Street
Birmingham B3 2PB, UK.

ISBN 978-1-78588-868-7

www.packtpub.com

Credits

Author
Thodoris Greasidis

Reviewer
Aamir Afridi

Commissioning Editor
Neil Alexander

Acquisition Editor
Aaron Lazar

Content Development Editor
Riddhi Tuljapurkar

Technical Editor
Pramod Kumavat

Copy Editors
Trishya Hazare
Kevin McGowan

Project Coordinator
Sanchita Mandal

Proofreader
Safis Editing

Indexer
Rekha Nair

Graphics
Abhinash Sahu

Production Coordinator
Shantanu N. Zagade

Cover Work
Shantanu N. Zagade

About the Author

Thodoris Greasidis is a senior web engineer from Greece. He graduated with honors from the University of Thessaly, holds a polytechnic diploma in computer, networking, and communications engineering, and a master's degree in computer science. He is a full-stack developer, responsible for implementing large-scale web applications with intuitive interfaces and high-availability web services.

Thodoris is part of the Angular-UI team and has made many open source contributions, with a special interest in Mozilla projects. He is also an active member of the Athens AngularJS Meetup and a technical reviewer of *Mastering jQuery UI*, *Packt Publishing*.

He is a JavaScript enthusiast and loves bitwise operations. His interests also include NodeJS, Python, project scaffolding, automation, and artificial intelligence, especially multi-agent systems.

A big thanks to everyone who supported me and showed understanding for my limited free time while writing this book.

About the Reviewer

Aamir Afridi has been passionate about the Internet and web development since 2002. He holds a master's degree in e-commerce. Over the years that have followed, he has worked for various companies and provided frontend engineering, including mobile web apps and architecture services with a focus on semantic HTML, CSS, and JavaScript/jQuery and anything else he can get his hands on. He has contributed to JavaScript books as a technical reviewer. These days, he is exploring the microservices architecture with NodeJS, MongoDB, and ReactJS at www.tes.com. He blogs on http://aamirafridi.com.

www.PacktPub.com

eBooks, discount offers, and more

Did you know that Packt offers eBook versions of every book published, with PDF and ePub files available? You can upgrade to the eBook version at www.PacktPub.com and as a print book customer, you are entitled to a discount on the eBook copy. Get in touch with us at customercare@packtpub.com for more details.

At www.PacktPub.com, you can also read a collection of free technical articles, sign up for a range of free newsletters and receive exclusive discounts and offers on Packt books and eBooks.

https://www2.packtpub.com/books/subscription/packtlib

Do you need instant solutions to your IT questions? PacktLib is Packt's online digital book library. Here, you can search, access, and read Packt's entire library of books.

Why subscribe?

- Fully searchable across every book published by Packt
- Copy and paste, print, and bookmark content
- On demand and accessible via a web browser

Table of Contents

Preface

Since its introduction in 2006, the jQuery library has made DOM traversals and manipulations much easier. This has resulted in the appearance of Web pages with increasingly complex user interactions, thus contributing to the maturing of Web as a platform capable of supporting large application implementations.

This book presents a series of best practices that make the implementation of Web applications more efficient. Moreover, we will analyze the most important Design Patterns that Computer Science has to offer, which can be applied to Web development. In this way, we will learn how to utilize techniques that are thoroughly used and tested in other fields of programming, which were initially created as generic methods to model solutions of complex problems.

In jQuery Design Patterns, we will analyze how various Design Patterns are utilized in the implementation of jQuery and how they can be used to improve the organization of our implementations. By adopting the Design Patterns demonstrated in this book, you will be able to create better organized implementations that resolve large problem categories faster. Moreover, when used by a developer team, they can improve the communication between them and lead to homogenous implementation, where every part of the code is easily understood by others.

What this book covers

Chapter 1, A Refresher on jQuery and the Composite Pattern, will teach the reader how to write the code using the Composite Pattern and method chaining (Fluent Interface) by analyzing how they are used for the implementation of jQuery itself. It also demonstrates the Iterator Pattern that nicely pairs with the Composite Collection objects that jQuery returns.

Chapter 2, The Observer Pattern, will teach you how to respond to user actions using the Observer Pattern. It also demonstrates how to use Event Delegation as a way to reduce the memory consumption and complexity of the code that handles dynamically injected page elements. Finally, it will teach you how to emit and listen for Custom Events in order to achieve greater flexibility and code decoupling.

Chapter 3, The Publish/Subscribe Pattern, will teach you how to utilize the Pub/Sub Pattern to create a central point to emit and receive application-level events, as a way to decouple your code and business logic from the HTML that is used for presentation.

Chapter 4, Divide and Conquer with the Module Pattern, demonstrates and compares some of the most commonly used Module Patterns in the industry. It will teach you how to structure your application in small independent Modules using Namespacing, leading to expandable implementations that follow the Separation of Concerns principle.

Chapter 5, The Facade Pattern, will teach you how to use the Facade Pattern to wrap complex APIs into simpler ones that are a better match for the needs of your application. It also demonstrates how to change parts of your application, while keeping the same module-level APIs and avoid affecting the rest of your implementation.

Chapter 6, The Builder and Factory Patterns, explains the concepts of and the differences between the Builder and Factory Patterns. It will teach you how and when to use each of them, in order to improve the clarity of your code by abstracting the generation of complex results into separate dedicated methods.

Chapter 7, Asynchronous Control Flow Patterns, will explain how jQuery's Deferred and Promise APIs work and compare them with the classical Callbacks Pattern. You will learn how to use Promises to control the the execution of asynchronous procedures to run either in an order or parallel to each other.

Chapter 8, Mock Object Pattern, teaches you how to create and use Mock Objects and Services as a way to ease the development of your application and get a sense of its functionality, long before all its parts are completed.

Chapter 9, Client-side Templating, demonstrates how to use the Underscore.js and Handlebars.js templating libraries as a better and faster way to create complex HTML structures with JavaScript. Through this chapter, you will get an overview of their conventions, evaluate their features, and find the one that best matches your taste.

Chapter 10, Plugin and Widget Development Patterns, introduces the basic concepts and conventions of jQuery Plugin development and analyzes the most commonly used design patterns, so that you will be able to identify and use the best match for any use case.

Chapter 11, Optimization Patterns, guides you with the best tips to create a highly efficient and robust implementation. You will be able to use this chapter as a checklist of best practices that improve the performance and lower the memory consumption of your applications, before moving them to a production environment.

What you need for this book

In order to run the examples in this book, you will need to have a web server installed on your system to serve the code files. For example, you can use Apache or IIS or NGINX. In order to make the installation process of Apache easier, you can use more complete development environment solutions, such as XAMPP or WAMP Server.

In terms of technical proficiency, this book assumes that you already have some experience of working with jQuery, HTML, CSS, and JSON. All the code samples in the book use jQuery v2.2.0 and some of the chapters also discuss the respective implementation in jQuery v1.12.0, which can be used in case support for older browsers is needed.

Who this book is for

This book targets existing jQuery developers or new developers who want to take their skills and understanding to an advanced level. It is a detailed introduction to how the various industry standard patterns can be applied to jQuery applications, and along with a set of the best practices, it can help large teams collaborate and create well organized and extendable implementations.

Conventions

In this book, you will find a number of text styles that distinguish between different kinds of information. Here are some examples of these styles and an explanation of their meaning.

Code words in text, folder names, filenames, file extensions, pathnames, dummy URLs, user input, and Twitter handles are shown as follows: "In the preceding CSS code, we first defined some basic styles for the `box`, `boxsizer`, and `clear` CSS classes."

A block of code is set as follows:

```
$.each([3, 5, 7], function(index){
    console.log(this + 1 + '!');
});
```

When we wish to draw your attention to a particular part of a code block, the relevant lines or items are set in bold:

```
$('#categoriesSelector').change(function() {
    var $selector = $(this);
    var message = { categoryID: $selector.val() };
    broker.trigger('dashboardCategorySelect', [message]);
});
```

We are following Google's JavaScript Style Guide, except from using four spaces for indentation, in order to improve the readability of the code in the book. In short, we are placing curly brackets on top and use single quotes for string literals.

> For more information on Google's JavaScript Style Guide you can visit the following URL: `https://google.github.io/styleguide/javascriptguide.xml`

Any command-line input or output is written as follows:

```
npm install jquery
```

New terms and **important words** are shown in bold. Words that you see on the screen, for example, in menus or dialog boxes, appear in the text like this: "The **jQuery Object** returned is an **Array-like object** that acts as a wrapper object and carries the collection of the retrieved elements."

> Warnings or important notes appear in a box like this.

> Tips and tricks appear like this.

Reader feedback

Feedback from our readers is always welcome. Let us know what you think about this book—what you liked or disliked. Reader feedback is important for us as it helps us develop titles that you will really get the most out of.

To send us general feedback, simply e-mail feedback@packtpub.com, and mention the book's title in the subject of your message.

If there is a topic that you have expertise in and you are interested in either writing or contributing to a book, see our author guide at www.packtpub.com/authors.

Customer support

Now that you are the proud owner of a Packt book, we have a number of things to help you to get the most from your purchase.

Downloading the example code

You can download the example code files from your account at http://www.packtpub.com for all the Packt Publishing books you have purchased. If you purchased this book elsewhere, you can visit http://www.packtpub.com/support and register to have the files e-mailed directly to you.

Errata

Although we have taken every care to ensure the accuracy of our content, mistakes do happen. If you find a mistake in one of our books—maybe a mistake in the text or the code—we would be grateful if you could report this to us. By doing so, you can save other readers from frustration and help us improve subsequent versions of this book. If you find any errata, please report them by visiting http://www.packtpub.com/submit-errata, selecting your book, clicking on the **Errata Submission Form** link, and entering the details of your errata. Once your errata are verified, your submission will be accepted and the errata will be uploaded to our website or added to any list of existing errata under the Errata section of that title.

To view the previously submitted errata, go to https://www.packtpub.com/books/content/support and enter the name of the book in the search field. The required information will appear under the **Errata** section.

Piracy

Piracy of copyrighted material on the Internet is an ongoing problem across all media. At Packt, we take the protection of our copyright and licenses very seriously. If you come across any illegal copies of our works in any form on the Internet, please provide us with the location address or website name immediately so that we can pursue a remedy.

Please contact us at copyright@packtpub.com with a link to the suspected pirated material.

We appreciate your help in protecting our authors and our ability to bring you valuable content.

Questions

If you have a problem with any aspect of this book, you can contact us at questions@packtpub.com, and we will do our best to address the problem.

1
A Refresher on jQuery and the Composite Pattern

Until the **Web 2.0** era started, the Web was just a document-based media and all it offered was just interconnecting different pages/documents and client-side scripting that was mostly limited to form validation. By 2005, Gmail and Google Maps were released, and JavaScript proved itself as a language used by big enterprises to create large-scale applications and provide rich user interface interactions.

Even though JavaScript has had very few changes since its original release, there was a tremendous change in the expectations that the Enterprise world had about what web pages should be capable of doing. Since then, web developers were required to deliver complex user interactions and, finally, the term "web application" appeared on the market. As a result, it started to become obvious that they should create some code abstractions, define some best practices, and adopt all the applicable **Design Patterns** that computer science had to offer. The wide adoption of JavaScript for enterprise-grade applications helped the evolution of the language, which with the **EcmaScript2015/EcmaScript6 (ES6)** specification was expanded in a way that allowed even more Design Patterns to be easily utilized.

In August 2006, the jQuery library was first released by John Resig at `http://jquery.com`, as an effort to create a convenient API to locate DOM elements. Since then, it has been an integral part of a web developer's toolkit. jQuery in its core uses several Design Patterns and tries to urge their use to the developer through the methods that it provides. The Composite Pattern is one of them and it is exposed to the developer through the very core `jQuery()` method, which is used for DOM traversal, one of the highlights of the jQuery library.

In this chapter, we will:

- Have a refresher on DOM scripting using jQuery
- Introduce the Composite Pattern
- See how the Composite Pattern is used by jQuery
- Discuss the gains offered by jQuery over plain JavaScript DOM manipulations
- Introduce the Iterator Pattern
- Use the Iterator Pattern in an example application

jQuery and DOM scripting

By DOM scripting, we refer to any procedure that alters or manipulates the elements of a web page after it has been loaded by the browser. The DOM API is a JavaScript API that was standardized in 1998 and it provides to web developers a collection of methods that allow the manipulation of the DOM tree elements that the browser creates after loading and parsing the web page's HTML code.

 For more information on the **Document Object Mode (DOM)** and its APIs, you can visit `https://developer.mozilla.org/en-US/docs/Web/API/Document_Object_Model/Introduction`.

By utilizing the DOM API in their JavaScript code, web developers can manipulate the DOM's nodes and add new elements or remove existing elements from the page. The primary use case for DOM scripting was initially limited to client-side form validation, but as the years passed and JavaScript gained the trust of the Enterprise world, more complex user interactions started to be implemented.

The initial version of the jQuery library was first released in August 2006 and it tried to ease the way the web developers were traversing and manipulating the DOM tree. One of its main goals was to provide abstractions that resulted in shorter, easier-to-read, and less error-prone code, while also ensuring cross-browser interoperability.

These core principles that jQuery follows are clearly visible in its homepage, where it presents itself as:

...a fast, small, and feature-rich JavaScript library. It makes things like HTML document traversal and manipulation, event handling, animation, and Ajax much simpler with an easy-to-use API that works across a multitude of browsers. With a combination of versatility and extensibility, jQuery has changed the way that millions of people write JavaScript.

The abstracted APIs that jQuery provided from the beginning, and the way that different Design Patterns were orchestrated, led to wide acceptance among the web developers. As a result, the jQuery library is referenced by more than 60% of the most visited websites worldwide, according to several sources such as BuiltWith.com (`http://trends.builtwith.com/javascript/jQuery`).

Manipulating the DOM using jQuery

To have a refresher on jQuery, we will go through an example web page that does some simple DOM manipulations. In this example, we will load a simply structured page that initially looks like the following figure:

DOM Manipulations

Doing DOM Manipulations is easy with JS!
Doing DOM Manipulations is easy with JS!
Doing DOM Manipulations is easy with JS!
Doing DOM Manipulations is easy with JS!
Doing DOM Manipulations is easy with JS!

We will use some jQuery code to change the page's content and layout and, in order to make its effects clearly visible, we will set it to run about 700 milliseconds after the page has loaded. The result of our manipulations will look like the following figure:

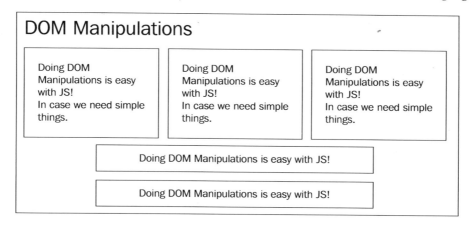

Now let's review the HTML code required for the preceding example:

```html
<!DOCTYPE html>
<html>
  <head>
    <title>DOM Manipulations</title>
    <link rel="stylesheet" type="text/css"
      href="dom-manipulations.css">
  </head>
  <body>
    <h1 id="pageHeader">DOM Manipulations</h1>

    <div class="boxContainer">
      <div>
        <p class="box">
          Doing DOM Manipulations is easy with JS!
        </p>
      </div>
      <div>
        <p class="box">
          Doing DOM Manipulations is easy with JS!
        </p>
      </div>
      <div>
        <p class="box">
          Doing DOM Manipulations is easy with JS!
        </p>
      </div>
    </div>

    <p class="box">
      Doing DOM Manipulations is easy with JS!
    </p>
    <p class="box">
      Doing DOM Manipulations is easy with JS!
    </p>

    <script type="text/javascript"
      src="https://code.jquery.com/jquery-2.2.0.min.js"></script>
    <script type="text/javascript"
      src="jquery-dom-manipulations.js"></script>
  </body>
</html>
```

The CSS code used is quite simple, containing only three CSS classes as follows:

```css
.box {
    padding: 7px 10px;
    border: solid 1px #333;
    margin: 5px 3px;
    box-shadow: 0 1px 2px #777;
}

.boxsizer {
    float: left;
    width: 33.33%;
}

.clear { clear: both; }
```

The preceding code results in a page looking like the first figure when opened in a browser and before our JavaScript code is executed. In the preceding CSS code, we first defined some basic styles for the box, boxsizer, and clear CSS classes. The box class styles the associated elements found in the page by using some padding, a thin border, some margin around, and a small shadow below the elements in order to make them look like a box. The boxsizer class will make the elements that use it to take just 1/3rd of the width of their parent element and create a three-column layout. Finally, the clear class will be used on an element as a break point for the column layout so that all the elements that follow will be positioned below it. The boxsizer and clear classes are not initially used by any element defined in the HTML code, but will be used after the DOM manipulations that we will do in JavaScript.

In the <body> element of our HTML, we initially define an <h1> heading element with ID pageHeader so that it is easily selectable through JavaScript. Right below it, we define five paragraph elements (<p>) with the box class, having the first three of them wrapped inside the three <div> elements and then inside another <div> element with the boxContainer class.

Reaching our two <script> tags, we first include a reference to the jQuery library from jQuery CDN. For more information, you can visit http://code.jquery.com/. In the second <script> tag, we reference the JavaScript file with the required code, for this example, which looks as follows:

```javascript
setTimeout(function() {
    $('#pageHeader').css('font-size', '3em');

    var $boxes = $('.boxContainer .box');
    $boxes.append(
      '<br /><br /><i>In case we need simple things</i>.');
```

```
        $boxes.parent().addClass('boxsizer');

        $('.boxContainer').append('<div class="clear">');
    }, 700);
```

All our code is wrapped inside a `setTimeout` call to delay its execution, according to the use case described earlier. The first parameter of the `setTimeout` function call is an anonymous function that will be executed after a timer of 700 milliseconds has expired, as defined in the second argument.

At the first line of our anonymous callback function, we use the jQuery `$()` function to traverse the DOM and locate the element with the ID `pageHeader`, and use the `css()` method to increase its `font-size` to `3em`. Next we provide a more complex CSS selector to the `$()` function, to locate all the elements with the `box` class that are descendants of the element with the `boxContainer` class, and then store the result in a variable named `$boxes`.

Variable naming conventions

It is a common practice among developers to use naming conventions for variables that hold objects of a certain type. Using such conventions not only helps you remember what the variable is holding, but also makes your code easier to understand by other developers of your team. Among jQuery developers, it is common to use variable names starting with a "$" sign when the variable stores the result of the `$()` function (also know as a jQuery collection object).

After we get a hold of the `box` elements that we are interested in, we append two breaking spaces and some extra text in italics, at the end of each of them. Then, we use the `$boxes` variable and traverse the DOM tree one level up, using the `parent()` method. The `parent()` method returns a different jQuery object holding the parent `<div>` elements of our initially selected boxes and then we chain a call to the `addClass()` method to assign them the `boxsizer` CSS class.

If you need to traverse all the parent nodes of a selected element, you can use the `$.fn.parents()` method. If you just need to find the first ancestor element that matches a given CSS selector, consider using the `$.fn.closest()` method instead.

Finally, since the `boxsizer` class uses floats to achieve the three-column layout, we need to clear the floats in the `boxContainer`. Once again, we traverse the DOM using the simple `.boxContainer` CSS selector and the `$()` function. Then, we call the `.append()` method to create a new `<div>` element with the `.clear` CSS class and insert it at the end of the `boxContainer`.

After 700 milliseconds, our jQuery code will have finished, resulting in the three-column layout as shown earlier. In its final state, the HTML code of our `boxContainer` element will look as follows:

```html
<div class="boxContainer">
  <div class="boxsizer">
    <p class="box">
      Doing DOM Manipulations is easy with JS!
      <br><br><i>In case we need simple things</i>.
    </p>
  </div>
  <div class="boxsizer">
    <p class="box">
      Doing DOM Manipulations is easy with JS!
      <br><br><i>In case we need simple things</i>.
    </p>
  </div>
  <div class="boxsizer">
    <p class="box">
      Doing DOM Manipulations is easy with JS!
      <br><br><i>In case we need simple things</i>.
    </p>
  </div>
  <div class="clear"></div>
</div>
```

Method Chaining and Fluent Interfaces

Actually, in the preceding example, we can also go one step further and combine all three box-related code statements into just one, which looks something as follows:

```js
$('.boxContainer .box')
  .append('<br /><br /><i>In case we need simple things</i>.')
  .parent()
  .addClass('boxsizer');
```

This Syntax Pattern is called **Method Chaining** and it is highly recommended by jQuery and the JavaScript community in general. Method Chaining is part of the Object Oriented Implementation Pattern of Fluent Interfaces where each method relays its instruction context to the subsequent one.

Most jQuery methods that apply on a jQuery object also return the same or a new jQuery element collection object. This allows us to chain several methods, not only resulting in a more readable and expressive code but also reducing the required variable declarations.

The Composite Pattern

The key concept of the Composite Pattern is to enable us to treat a collection of objects in the same way as we treat a single object instance. Manipulating a composition by using a method on the collection will result in applying the manipulation to each part of it. Such methods can be applied successfully, regardless of the number of elements that are part of the composite collection, or even when the collection contains no elements.

Also, the objects of a composite collection do not necessarily have to provide the exact same methods. The Composite Object can either expose only the methods that are common among the objects of the collection, or can provide an abstracted API and appropriately handle the method differentiations of each object.

Let's continue by exploring how the intuitive API that jQuery exposes is highly influenced from the Composite Pattern.

How the Composite Pattern is used by jQuery

The Composite Pattern is an integral part of jQuery's architecture and is applied from the very core $() function itself. Each call to the $() function creates and returns an element collection object, which is often simply referred as a jQuery object. This is exactly where we see the first principle of the Composite Patterns; in fact, instead of returning a single element, the $() function returns a collection of elements.

The jQuery object returned is an Array-like object that acts as a wrapper object and carries the collection of the retrieved elements. It also exposes a number of extra properties as follows:

- The `length` of the retrieved element collection
- The `context` that the object was constructed

- The CSS `selector` that was used on the `$()` function call

- A `prevObject` property in case we need to access the previous element collection after chaining a method call

Simple Array-like object definition

An Array-like object is a JavaScript object { } that has a numeric `length` property and the respective number of properties, with sequential numeric property names. In other words, an Array-like object that has the `length == 2` property is expected to also have two properties defined, `"0"` and `"1"`. Given the above properties, Array-like objects allow you to access their content using simple `for` loops, by utilizing JavaScript's Bracket Property Accessor's syntax:

```
for (var i = 0; i < obj.length; i++) {
   console.log(obj[i]);
}
```

We can easily experiment with the jQuery objects returned from the `$()` function and inspect the properties described above, by using the developer tools of our favorite browser. To open the developer tools on most of them, we just need to press *F12* on Windows and Linux or *Cmd + Opt + I* on Mac, and right after that, we can issue some `$()` calls in the console and click on the returned objects to inspect their properties.

In the following figure, we can see what the result of the `$('#pageHeader')` call, which we used in the example earlier, looks like in Firefox Developer Tools:

```
$('#pageHeader')                                          ▼ Object
Object { 0: <h1#pageHeader> , length: 1, context:          ▶ 0: <h1#pageHeader>
HTMLDocument → jQuery%20DOM%20Manipulations.html,          ▶ context: HTMLDocument → jQuery%20DOM%20Manipulations.html
selector: "#pageHeader" }                                    length: 1
                                                             selector: "#pageHeader"
                                                           ▶ __proto__: Object
```

The result of the `$('.boxContainer .box')` call looks as follows:

```
$('.boxContainer .box')                                   ▼ Object
Object { 0: <p.box> , 1: <p.box> , 2: <p.box> ,            ▶ 0: <p.box>
length: 3, prevObject: Object, context: HTMLDocument       ▶ 1: <p.box>
→ jQuery%20DOM%20Manipulations.html, selector:             ▶ 2: <p.box>
".boxContainer .box" }                                     ▶ context: HTMLDocument → jQuery%20DOM%20Manipulations.html
                                                             length: 3
                                                           ▶ prevObject: Object
                                                             selector: ".boxContainer .box"
                                                           ▶ __proto__: Object
```

The fact that jQuery uses Array-like objects as a wrapper for the returned elements allows it to expose some extra methods that apply on the collection returned. This is achieved through prototypical inheritance of the `jQuery.fn` object, resulting in each jQuery object also having access to all the methods that jQuery provides. This completes the Composite Pattern, which provides methods that, when applied to a collection, are appropriately applied to each of its members. Because jQuery uses Array-like objects with prototypical inheritance, these methods can be easily accessed as properties on each jQuery object, as shown in the example in the beginning of the chapter: `$('#pageHeader').css('font-size', '3em');`. Moreover, jQuery adds some extra goodies to its DOM manipulating code, following the goal of smaller and less error-prone code. For example, when using the `jQuery.fn.html()` method to change the inner HTML of a DOM node that already contains child elements, jQuery first tries to remove any data and event handlers that are associated with the child elements, before removing them from the page and appending the provided HTML code.

Let's take a look at how jQuery implements these collection-applicable methods. For this task, we can either download and view the source code from the GitHub page of jQuery (`https://github.com/jquery/jquery/releases`), or we can use a tool such as the jQuery Source Viewer that is available at `http://james.padolsey.com/jquery`.

 Depending on the version you are using, you might get different results to some degree. The most recent stable jQuery version that was released and used as a reference while writing this book, was v2.2.0.

One of the simplest methods to demonstrate how methods that apply to collections are implemented, is `jQuery.fn.empty()`. You can easily locate its implementation in jQuery's source code by searching for `"empty:"` or using the jQuery Source Viewer and searching for `"jQuery.fn.empty"`. Using either one of the ways will bring us to the following code:

```
empty: function() {
  var elem, i = 0;

  for ( ; ( elem = this[ i ] ) != null; i++ ) {
    if ( elem.nodeType === 1 ) {
      // Prevent memory leaks
      jQuery.cleanData( getAll( elem, false ) );

      // Remove any remaining nodes
      elem.textContent = "";
```

```
        }
    }

    return this;
}
```

As you can see, the code is not complex at all. jQuery iterates over all the items of the collection object (referred to as `this` since we are inside the method implementation) by using a plain `for` loop. For each item of the collection, that is, an Element Node, it clears any data-* property values using the `jQuery.cleanData()` helper function, and right after this, it clears its content by setting it to an empty string.

 For more information on the different specified Node Types, you can visit `https://developer.mozilla.org/en-US/docs/Web/API/Node/nodeType`.

Comparing the benefits over the plain DOM API

To clearly demonstrate the benefits that the Composite Pattern provides, we will rewrite our initial example without the abstractions that jQuery offers. By using just plain JavaScript and the DOM API, we can write an equivalent code that looks as follows:

```
setTimeout(function() {
  var headerElement = document.getElementById('pageHeader');
  if (headerElement) {
    headerElement.style.fontSize = '3em';
  }
  var boxContainerElement =
      document.getElementsByClassName('boxContainer')[0];
  if (boxContainerElement) {
    var innerBoxElements =
        boxContainerElement.getElementsByClassName('box');
    for (var i = 0; i < innerBoxElements.length; i++) {
      var boxElement = innerBoxElements[i];
      boxElement.innerHTML +=
          '<br /><br /><i>In case we need simple things</i>.';
      boxElement.parentNode.className += ' boxsizer';
    }
```

```
        var clearFloatDiv = document.createElement('div');
        clearFloatDiv.className = 'clear';
        boxContainerElement.appendChild(clearFloatDiv);
    }
}, 700);
```

Once again, we use `setTimeout` with an anonymous function and set `700` milliseconds as the second parameter. Inside the function itself, we use `document.getElementById` to retrieve elements that are known to have a unique ID in the page, and later `document.getElementsByClassName` when we need to retrieve all the elements that have a specific class. We also use `boxContainerElement.getElementsByClassName('box')` to retrieve all the elements with the `box` class that are descendants of the element with the `boxContainer` class.

The most obvious observation is that, in this case, we needed 18 lines of code in order to achieve the same results. For comparison, when using jQuery, we only needed 9 lines of code, that's half the number of lines of code compared to the later implementation. Using the jQuery `$()` function with a CSS selector was an easier way to retrieve the elements that we needed, and it also ensures compatibility with browsers that do not support the `getElementsByClassName()` method. However, there are more benefits than just the code line count and the improved readability. As an implementer of the Composite Pattern, the `$()` function always retrieves element collections, making our code more uniform when compared to the differentiated handling of each `getElement*` method we used. We use the `$()` function in exactly the same way, regardless of whether we just want to retrieve an element with a unique ID or a number of elements with a specific class.

As an extra benefit of returning Array-like objects, jQuery can also provide more convenient methods to traverse and manipulate the DOM, such as those we saw in our first example, `.css()`, `.append()` and `.parent()`, which are accessible as properties of the returned object. Additionally, jQuery also offers methods that abstract more complex use cases such as `.addClass()` and `.wrap()` that have no equivalent methods available as part of the DOM API.

Since the returned jQuery collection objects do not differ in anything other than the elements they wrap, we can use any method of the jQuery API in the same way. As we saw earlier, these methods apply to each element of the retrieved collection, regardless of the element count. As a result, we do not need a separate `for` loop to iterate over each retrieved element and apply our manipulations individually; instead, we apply our manipulations (for example, `.addClass()`) directly to the collection object.

To continue providing the same execution safety guaranties in the later example, we also need to add some extra `if` statements to check for `null` values. This is required because, for example, if the `headerElement` is not found, an error will occur and the rest of the lines of code will never be executed. Someone could argue that these checks, such as `if (headerElement)` and `if (boxContainerElement)`, are not required in this example and can be omitted. This might appear to be correct in this example, but actually this is among the top reasons for errors while developing large-scale applications, where elements are created, inserted, and removed from the DOM tree continuously. Unfortunately, programmers in all languages and target platforms tend to first write their implementation logic and fill such checks at a later time, often after they get an error when testing their implementation.

Following the Composite Pattern, even an empty jQuery collection object (one that contains no retrieved elements) is still a valid collection object, where we can safely apply any method that jQuery provides. As a result, we do not need the extra `if` statements to check whether a collection actually contains any element before applying a method such as `.css()`, just for the sake of avoiding a JavaScript runtime error.

Overall, the abstractions that jQuery offers by using the Composite Pattern lead to fewer lines of code, which is more readable, uniform, and with fewer typo-prone lines (compare typing `$('#elementID')` versus `document.getElementById('elementID')`).

Using the Composite Pattern to develop applications

Now that we have seen how jQuery uses the Composite Pattern in its architecture and also did a comparison on the benefits it provided, let's try to write an example use case of our own. We will try to cover all concepts that we have seen earlier in this chapter. We will structure our Composite to be an Array-like object, operate on totally different structured objects, provide a Fluent API to allow chaining, and have methods that apply on all the items of the collection.

A sample use case

Let's say that we have an application that at some point needs to perform operations on numbers. On the other hand, the items that it needs to operate on come from different sources and are not uniform at all. To make this example interesting, let's suppose that one source of data provides plain numbers and another one provides objects with a specific property that holds the number we are interested in:

```
var numberValues = [2, 5, 8];

var objectsWithValues = [
    { value: 7 },
    { value: 4 },
    { value: 6 },
    { value: 9 }
];
```

The objects returned by the second source of our use case could have a more complex structure and probably some extra properties. Such changes wouldn't differentiate our example implementation in any way, since when developing a Composite we are only interested in providing a uniform handling over the common parts between the targeted items.

The Composite Collection Implementation

Let's proceed and define the Constructor Function and the prototype that will describe our Composite Collection Object:

```
function ValuesComposite() {
    this.length = 0;
}

ValuesComposite.prototype.append = function(item) {
    if ((typeof item === 'object' && 'value' in item) ||
        typeof item === 'number') {
        this[this.length] = item;
        this.length++;
    }

    return this;
};

ValuesComposite.prototype.increment = function(number) {
    for (var i = 0; i < this.length; i++) {
        var item = this[i];
```

```
            if (typeof item === 'object' && 'value' in item) {
                item.value += number;
            } else if (typeof item === 'number') {
                this[i] += number;
            }
        }
    }

    return this;
};


ValuesComposite.prototype.getValues = function() {
    var result = [];
    for (var i = 0; i < this.length; i++) {
        var item = this[i];
        if (typeof item === 'object' && 'value' in item) {
            result.push(item.value);
        } else if (typeof item === 'number') {
            result.push(item);
        }
    }
    return result;
};
```

The `ValuesComposite()` constructor function in our example is quite simple. When invoked with the `new` operator, it returns an empty object with a `length` property equal to zero, representing that the collection it wraps is empty.

> For more information on the Prototype-based programming model of JavaScript, visit `https://developer.mozilla.org/en-US/docs/Web/JavaScript/Introduction_to_Object-Oriented_JavaScript`.

We first need to define a way that will enable us to populate our composite collection objects. We defined the `append` method that checks whether the provided parameter is one of the types that it can handle; in this case, it appends the parameter on the Composite Object on the next available numeric property and increments the `length` property value. For example, the first appended item, whether it is an object with a value property or a plain number, will be exposed to the "0" property of the Composite Object and will be accessible with the Bracket Property Accessor's syntax as `myValuesComposition[0]`.

The `increment` method is presented as a simple example method that can manipulate such collections by operating over all the collection items. It accepts a numeric value as a parameter and then appropriately handles it by adding it to each item of our collection, based on their type. Since our composite is an Array-like object, `increment` uses a `for` loop to iterate over all the collection items and either increases the `item.value` (in case the item is an object) or the actual numeric value stored (when the collection item stored is a number). In the same manner, we can continue and implement other methods that will, for example, enable us to multiply the collection items with a specific number.

In order to allow chaining the methods of our Composite Object, all the methods of the prototype need to return a reference to the instance of the object. We achieve this goal by simply adding a `return this;` statement as the last line for all the methods that manipulate the collection, such as `append` and `increment`. Keep in mind that methods such as `getValues` that do not manipulate the collection but are used to return a result, by definition, can't be chained to relay the collection object instance to subsequent method calls.

Finally, we implement the `getValues` method as a convenient way to retrieve the actual numeric values of all the items in our collection. Similar to the `increment` method, the `getValues` method abstracts away the handling between the different item types of our collection. It iterates over the collection items, extracts each numeric value, and appends them to a `result` array that it returns to its caller.

An example execution

Let's now see an actual example that will use the Composite Object we just implemented:

```
var valuesComposition = new ValuesComposite();

for (var i = 0; i < numberValues.length; i++) {
    valuesComposition.append(numberValues[i]);
}

for (var i = 0; i < objectsWithValues.length; i++) {
    valuesComposition.append(objectsWithValues[i]);
}

valuesComposition.increment(2)
    .append(1)
    .append(2)
    .append({ value: 3 });

console.log(valuesComposition.getValues());
```

When the preceding code is executed in a browser, by writing the code either in an existing page or directly in the browser's console, it will log a result that looks as follows:

▶ `Array [ 4, 7, 10, 9, 6, 8, 11, 1, 2, 3 ]`

We are using our data sources such as the `numberValues` and `objectsWithValues` variables that were shown earlier. The preceding code iterates over both of them and appends their items to a newly created Composite Object instance. We then proceed by incrementing the values of our composite collection by 2. Right after this, we chain the three item insertions using `append`, with the first two appending numeric values and the third appending an object with a value property. Finally, we use the `getValues` method in order to get an array with all the numeric values of our collection and log it in our browser's console.

Alternative implementations

Keep in mind that a Composite does not need to be an Array-like object, but is commonly preferred since JavaScript makes it easy to create such an implementation. Additionally, Array-like implementations also have the benefit of allowing us to iterate over the collection items using a simple `for` loop.

On the other hand, in case an Array-like object is not preferred, we can easily use a property on the Composite Object to hold our collection items. For example, this property can be named as `items` and be used to store and access the items of the collection inside our methods using `this.items.push(item)` and `this.items[i]`, respectively.

The Iterator Pattern

The key concept of the Iterator Pattern is the use of a function with the single responsibility to traverse a collection and provide access to its items. This function is known as the iterator and provides a way to access the items of the collection, without exposing implementation specifics and the underlying data structure used by the collection object.

Iterators provide a level of encapsulation regarding the way the iteration occurs, decoupling the iteration over the items of a collection from the implementation logic of their consumers.

For more information on the **Single Responsibility principle**, you can visit `http://www.oodesign.com/single-responsibility-principle.html`.

How the Iterator Pattern is used by jQuery

As we saw earlier in this chapter, the jQuery core `$()` function returns an Array-like object that wraps a collection of page elements and it also provides an iterator function to traverse it and access each element individually. It actually goes one step further and provides a generic helper method `jQuery.each()` that can iterate over arrays, Array-like objects, and also object properties.

A more technical description can be found in jQuery API documentation page at `http://api.jquery.com/jQuery.each/`, where the description of `jQuery.each()` reads as follows:

> *A generic iterator function, which can be used to seamlessly iterate over both objects and arrays. Arrays and Array-like objects with a length property (such as a function's arguments object) are iterated by numeric index, from 0 to length-1. Other objects are iterated via their named properties.*

The `jQuery.each()` helper function is used internally in several places of the jQuery source code. One of its uses is iterating over the items of a jQuery object and applying manipulations on each of them, as the Composite Pattern suggests. A simple search for the keyword `.each(` reveals 56 matches.

As of writing this book, the latest stable version is v2.2.0 and this was used for the above statistics.

We can easily trace its implementation in jQuery's source, either by searching for `"each:"` (note that there are two occurrences) or using the jQuery Source Viewer and searching for `"jQuery.each()"` (like we did earlier in this chapter):

```
each: function( obj, callback ) {
  var length, i = 0;

  if ( isArrayLike( obj ) ) {
    length = obj.length;
```

```
        for ( ; i < length; i++ ) {
          if ( callback.call( obj[ i ], i, obj[ i ] ) === false ) {
            break;
          }
        }
      } else {
        for ( i in obj ) {
          if ( callback.call( obj[ i ], i, obj[ i ] ) === false ) {
            break;
          }
        }
      }

      return obj;
    }
```

This helper function is also accessible on any jQuery object by using the same prototypical inheritance that we saw earlier for methods such as .append(). You can easily find the code that does exactly this, by searching for "jQuery.fn.each()" in jQuery Source Viewer or directly searching jQuery source code for each: (note that there are two occurrences):

```
each: function( callback ) {
  return jQuery.each( this, callback );
}
```

Using the method version of ".each()" enables us to directly iterate over the elements of a jQuery collection object with a more convenient syntax.

The example code that follows showcases how the two flavors of .each() can be used in our code:

```
// using the helper function on an array
$.each([3, 5, 7], function(index){
    console.log(this + 1);
});
// using the method on a jQuery object
$('.boxContainer .box').each(function(index) {
    console.log('I\'m box #' + (index + 1)); // index is zero-based
});
```

When executed, the preceding code will log the following on the browser's console:

```
4
6
8
I'm box #1
I'm box #2
I'm box #3
```

How it pairs with the Composite Pattern

Since the Composite Pattern encapsulates a collection of items into a single object and the Iterator Pattern can be used to iterate over an abstracted data structure, we can easily characterize these two patterns as complementary.

Where can it be used

The Iterator Pattern can be used in our applications to abstract the way we access items from a data structure. For example, let's suppose we need to retrieve all the items that are greater than 4 from the following tree structure:

```
var collection = {
    nodeValue: 7,
    left: {
        nodeValue: 4,
        left: 2,
        right: {
            nodeValue: 6,
            left: 5,
            right: 9
        }
    },
    right: {
        nodeValue: 9,
        left: 8
    }
};
```

Let's now implement our iterator function. Since tree data structures can have nesting, we end up with the following recursive implementation:

```
function iterateTreeValues(node, callback) {
    if (node === null || node === undefined) {
        return;
    }

    if (typeof node === 'object') {
        if ('left' in node) {
            iterateTreeValues(node.left, callback);
        }
        if ('nodeValue' in node) {
            callback(node.nodeValue);
        }
        if ('right' in node) {
            iterateTreeValues(node.right, callback);
        }
    } else {
        // its a leaf, so the node is the value
        callback(node);
    }
}
```

Finally, we end up with an implementation that looks as follows:

```
var valuesArray = [];
iterateTreeValues(collection, function(value) {
    if (value > 4) {
        valuesArray.push(value);
    }
});
console.log(valuesArray);
```

When executed, the preceding code will log the following on the browser's console:

```
▶ Array [ 5, 6, 9, 7, 8, 9 ]
```

We can clearly see that the iterator simplified our code. We no longer bother with the implementation specifics of the data structure used every time we need to access some items that fulfill certain criteria. Our implementation works on top of the generic API that the iterator exposes, and our implementation logic appears in the callback that we provide to the iterator.

This encapsulation allows us to decouple our implementation from the data structure used, given that an iterator with the same API will be available. For instance, in this example, we can easily change the data structure used to a sorted binary tree or a simple array and preserve our implementation logic the same.

Summary

In this chapter, we had a refresher on JavaScript's DOM Scripting API and jQuery. We were introduced to the Composite Pattern and saw how it is used by the jQuery library. We saw how the Composite Pattern simplifies our workflow after we rewrote our example page without using jQuery, and later showcased an example of using the Composite Pattern in our applications. Finally, we were introduced to the Iterator Pattern and saw how well it pairs when used along with the Composite Pattern.

Now that we have completed our introduction on how the Composite Pattern plays an important role in the way we use jQuery methods every day, we can move on to the next chapter where we will showcase the Observer Pattern and the convenient way to utilize it in our pages using jQuery.

2
The Observer Pattern

In this chapter, we will showcase the Observer Pattern and the convenient way in which we can utilize it in our pages using jQuery. Later on, we will also explain the Delegated Event Observer Pattern variant, which when properly applied to web pages can lead to code simplifications and also lessen the memory consumption that a page requires.

In this chapter, we will:

- Introduce the Observer Pattern
- See how the Observer Pattern is used by jQuery
- Compare the Observer Pattern with using the event attributes
- Learn how to avoid memory leaks from observers
- Introduce the Delegated Event Observer Pattern and showcasing its benefits

Introducing the Observer Pattern

The key concept of the Observer Pattern is that there is an object, often referred to as the observable or the subject, whose internal state changes during its lifetime. There are also several other objects, referred as the observers, that want to be notified in the event that the state of the observable/subject changes, in order to execute some operations.

The observers may need to be notified about any kind of state change of the observable or only specific types of changes. In the most common implementation, the observable maintains a list with its observers and notifies them when an appropriate state change occurs. In case a state change occurs to the observable, it iterates through the list of observers that are interested for that type of state change and executes a specific method that they have defined.

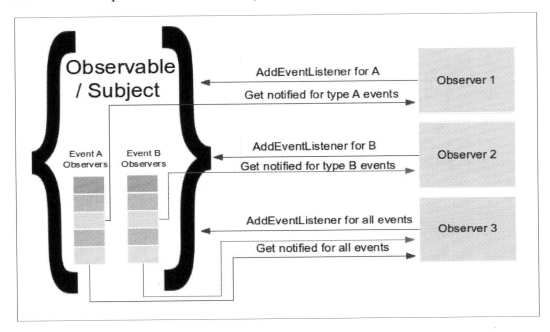

According to the definition of the Observer Pattern and the reference implementation in Computer Science books, the observers are described as objects that implement a well-known programming interface, in most cases, specific to each observable they are interested in. In the case of a state change, the observable will execute the well-known method of each observer as it is defined in the programming interface.

> For more information on how the Observer Pattern is used in traditional, object-oriented programming, you can visit http://www.oodesign. com/observer-pattern.html.

In the web stack, the Observer Pattern often uses plain anonymous callback functions as observers instead of objects with well-known methods. An equivalent result, as defined by the Observer Pattern, can be achieved since the callback function keeps references to the variables of the environment that it was defined in—a pattern commonly referenced as a **Closure**. The main benefit of using the Observer Pattern over callbacks as invocation or initialization parameters is that the Observer Pattern can support several independent handlers on a single target.

 For more information on closures, you can visit `https://developer.mozilla.org/en-US/docs/Web/JavaScript/Closures`.

Defining a simple callback

A callback can be defined as a function that is passed as an argument to another function/method or is assigned to a property of an object and expected to be executed at some later point of time. In this way, the piece of code that was handed our callback will invoke or call it, propagating the results of an operation or event back to the context where the callback was defined.

Since the pattern of registering functions as observers has proven to be more flexible and straightforward to program, it can be found in programming languages outside the web stack as well. Other programming languages provide an equivalent functionality through language features or special objects such as subroutines, lambda expressions, blocks, and function pointers. For example, Python also defines functions as first-class objects such as JavaScript, enabling them to be used as callbacks, while C# defines Delegates as a special object type in order to achieve the same result.

The Observer Pattern is an integral part of developing web interfaces that respond to user actions, and every web developer has used it to some degree, even without noticing it. This is because the first thing that a web developer needs to do while creating a rich user interface is to add event listeners to page elements and define how the browser should respond to them.

This is traditionally achieved by using the `EventTarget.addEventListener()` method on the page elements that we need to listen to for events such as a "click", and providing a callback function with the code that needs to be executed when that event occurs. It is worth mentioning that in order to support older versions of Internet Explorer, testing for the existence of `EventTarget.attachEvent()`, and using that instead, is required.

For more information on the `addEventListener()` and `attachEvent()` methods, you can visit `https://developer.mozilla.org/en-US/docs/Web/API/EventTarget/addEventListener` and `https://developer.mozilla.org/en-US/docs/Web/API/EventTarget/attachEvent`.

How it is used by jQuery

The jQuery library heavily uses the Observer Pattern in several parts of its implementation, either directly by using the `addEventListener` method or creating its own abstraction over it. Moreover, jQuery offers a series of abstractions and convenient methods to make working with the Observer Pattern easier on the web and also uses some of them internally to implement other methods as well.

The jQuery on method

The `jQuery.fn.on()` method is the central jQuery method for attaching event handlers to elements, providing an easy way to adopt the Observer Pattern, while keeping our code easy to read and reason. It attaches the requested event handler over all the elements of a composite jQuery collection object returned by the `$()` function.

Searching for `jQuery.fn.on` in jQuery's Source Viewer (which is available at `http://james.padolsey.com/jquery`), or directly searching jQuery's source code for `on: function` (the first character is a tab), will lead us to the method's definition, which counts 67 lines of code. Actually, the first 55 lines of the internal on function are just handling all the different ways that the `jQuery.fn.on()` method can be invoked; near its end, we can see that it actually uses the internal method `jQuery.event.add()`:

```
jQuery.fn.extend({
  on: function( types, selector, data, fn ) {
    return on( this, types, selector, data, fn );
  }
});

function on( elem, types, selector, data, fn, one ) {

  /* 55 lines of code handling the method overloads */
  return elem.each( function() {
    jQuery.event.add( this, types, fn, data, selector );
  } );
}
```

The `jQuery.event` object is the one-place stop for event handling in jQuery and its implementation counts around 443 lines of code. It holds several helper functions for managing events such as `add`, `dispatch`, `fix`, `handlers`, `remove`, `simulate`, and `trigger`. All these functions are used internally by jQuery itself wherever the Observer Pattern appears or managing events is required.

Searching for `jQuery.event.add` in jQuery's Source Viewer or `jQuery.event =` directly in jQuery's source code, will lead us to the relatively long implementation of the helper function that counts around 107 lines of code in jQuery v2.2.0. The following code snippet shows a trimmed down version of that method, where some code related to the technical implementation of jQuery and not related to the Observer Pattern has been removed for clarity:

```
add: function( elem, types, handler, data, selector ) {
    /* ... 4 lines of code ... */
        elemData = dataPriv.get( elem );
    /* ... 13 lines of code ... */

    // Make sure that the handler has a unique ID,
    // used to find/remove it later
    if ( !handler.guid ) {
        handler.guid = jQuery.guid++;
    }

    // Init the element's event structure and main handler,
    // if this is the first
    if ( !( events = elemData.events ) ) {
        events = elemData.events = {};
    }
    /* ... 9 lines of code ... */

    // Handle multiple events separated by a space
    types = ( types || "" ).match( rnotwhite ) || [ "" ];
    t = types.length;
    while ( t-- ) {
        /* ... 30 lines of code ... */

        // Init the event handler queue if we're the first
        if ( !( handlers = events[ type ] ) ) {
            handlers = events[ type ] = [];
            handlers.delegateCount = 0;

            // Only use addEventListener if the special events handler
            // returns false
            if ( !special.setup || special.setup.call(
                elem, data, namespaces, eventHandle ) === false ) {
                if ( elem.addEventListener ) {
                    elem.addEventListener( type, eventHandle );
```

```
                    }
                }
            }

            /* ... 9 lines of code ... */

            // Add to the element's handler list, delegates in front
            if ( selector ) {
                handlers.splice( handlers.delegateCount++, 0,
                    handleObj );
            } else {
                handlers.push( handleObj );
            }
            /* ... 3 lines of code ... */
        }
    }
```

Now, let's see how the Observer Pattern is implemented by `jQuery.event.add()`, by referring to the preceding highlighted code.

The `handler` variable in the arguments of the `jQuery.event.add()` method stores the function that was originally passed as an argument to the `jQuery.fn.on()` method. We can refer to this function as our observer function, since it is executed when the appropriate event fires on the element that it was attached to.

In the first highlighted code area, jQuery creates and assigns a `guid` property to the observer function that is stored in the `handler` variable. Keep in mind that assigning properties to functions is possible in JavaScript, since functions are first-class objects. The `jQuery.guid++` statement is executed right after the assignment of the old value and is required since `jQuery.guid` is a page-wide counter used by jQuery and jQuery plugins internally. The `guid` property on the observer function is used as a way to identify and locate the observer function inside the observer list that jQuery has for each element. For example, it is used by the `jQuery.fn.off()` method to locate and remove an observer function from the observer list associated with an element.

jQuery.guid is a page-wide counter that is used by the plugins and jQuery itself as a centralized way to retrieve unique integer IDs. It is often used to assign unique IDs to elements, objects, and functions, in order to make it easier to locate them in collections. It is the responsibility of each implementer that retrieves and uses the current value of `jQuery.guid` to also increase the property value (by one) after each use. Otherwise, and since this is a page-wide counter that is used by both jQuery plugins and jQuery themselves for identification, the page will probably face malfunctions that are hard to debug.

In the second and third highlighted code areas, jQuery initializes an array to hold the observer lists for each individual event that may fire on that element. One thing to note in the second highlighted code area is that the observer lists found in the elemData variable are not a property on the actual DOM element. As shown in the dataPriv.get(elem) statement, near the start of the jQuery.event.add() method, jQuery uses separate mapping objects to hold the associations between DOM elements and their observer lists. By using this data cache mechanism, jQuery is able to avoid polluting the DOM elements with the extra properties that are needed by its implementation.

You can easily locate the data cache mechanism implementation in the source code of jQuery by searching for function Data(). This will bring you to the constructor function of the Data class that is also followed by the implementation of the class methods that are defined in the Data.prototype object. For more information, you can visit http://api.jquery.com/data.

The next highlighted code area is where jQuery checks whether the EventTarget.addEventListener() method is actually available for that element and then uses it to add the event listener to the element. In the final highlighted code area, jQuery adds the observer function to its internal list, which holds all the observers of the same event type that are attached to that specific element.

Depending on the version you are using, you might get different results to some degree. The most recent stable jQuery version released and used as reference while writing this book was v2.2.0.

In case you need to provide support for older browsers, for example, Internet Explorer lower than version 9, then you should use the v1.x versions of jQuery. The latest version as of the writing of this book was v1.12.0, which offers the exact same API as the v2.2.x versions, but also has the required code to work on older browsers.

In order to cover the implementation inconsistencies of older browsers, the implementation of jQuery.event.add() in jQuery v1.x is a bit longer and more complex. One of the reasons for this is because jQuery also needs to test whether EventTarget.addEventListener() is actually available in the browser that it is running and try to use EventTarget.attachEvent() if this is not the case.

As we saw in the preceding code, the jQuery implementation follows the operation model that the Observer Pattern describes, but it also incorporates some implementation tricks in order to make it work more efficiently with the APIs available to web browsers.

The document-ready observer

Another convenient method that jQuery offers, which is widely used by developers, is the `$.fn.ready()` method. This method accepts a function parameter and executes it only after the DOM tree of the page has been fully loaded. Such a thing can be useful in case your code is not loaded last in the page and you don't want to block the initial page render, or the elements that it needs to manipulate are defined later than its own `<script>` tag.

 Keep in mind that the `$.fn.ready()` method works slightly differently than the `window.onload` callback and the "load" event of the page, which wait until all the resources of the page are loaded. For more information, you can visit `http://api.jquery.com/ready`.

The following code demonstrates the most common way to use the `$.fn.ready()` method:

```
$(document).ready(function() {
    /* this code will execute only after the page has been fully
        loaded */
})
```

If we try to locate the implementation of `jQuery.fn.ready`, we will see that it actually uses `jQuery.ready.promise` internally to work:

```
jQuery.fn.ready = function( fn ) {
  // Add the callback
  jQuery.ready.promise().done( fn );

  return this;
};
/* … a lot lines of code in between */
jQuery.ready.promise = function( obj ) {
  if ( !readyList ) {

    readyList = jQuery.Deferred();


    // Catch cases where $(document).ready() is called
    // after the browser event has already occurred.
    // Support: IE9-10 only
    // Older IE sometimes signals "interactive" too soon
```

```
if ( document.readyState === "complete" ||
  ( document.readyState !== "loading" &&
  !document.documentElement.doScroll ) ) {
  // Handle it asynchronously to allow ... to delay ready
  window.setTimeout( jQuery.ready );

} else {
  // Use the handy event callback
  document.addEventListener( "DOMContentLoaded",
    completed );

  // A fallback to window.onload, that will always work
  window.addEventListener( "load", completed );
  }
}
  return readyList.promise( obj );
};
```

As you can see in the preceding highlighted code areas of the implementation, jQuery uses `addEventListener` to observe when the `DOMContentLoaded` event is fired on the `document` object. Moreover, to ensure that it will work across a wide range of browsers, it also observes for the `load` event to be fired on the `window` object.

The jQuery library also provides shorter methods to add the above functionality in your code. Since the aforementioned implementation does not actually need a reference to the document, we can instead just write `$().ready(function() {/* ... */ })`. There also exists an overload of the `$()` function that achieves the same result, which is used like `$(function() {/* ... */ })`. These two alternative ways to use `jQuery.fn.ready` have been heavily criticized among developers, since they commonly lead to misunderstandings. The second, shorter version in particular can lead to confusion, since it looks like an **Immediately Invoked Function Expression (IIFE)**, a pattern that JavaScript developers use heavily and have learned to recognize. In fact, it only differs by one character ($) and as a result, its use is not suggested before a discussion with the rest of your developer team.

> The `$.fn.ready()` method is also characterized as a method that provides an easy way to implement the Lazy Initialization/Execution Pattern in our code. The core concept of this pattern is to postpone the execution of a piece of code or load a remote resource at a later point of time. For example, we can wait for the page to be fully loaded until we add our observers or wait for a certain event to happen before downloading a web resource.

Demonstrate a sample use case

In order to see the Observer Pattern in action, we will create an example showcasing a skeleton implementation of a dashboard. In our example, the user will be able to add information boxes to his dashboard related to some sample items and categories that are available for selection on the header.

Our example will have three predefined categories for our items: **Products** , **Sales**, and **Advertisements**. Each of these categories will have a series of related items that will appear in the area right below the category selector. The user will be able to select the desired category by using a drop-down selector and this will change the visible selection items of the dashboard.

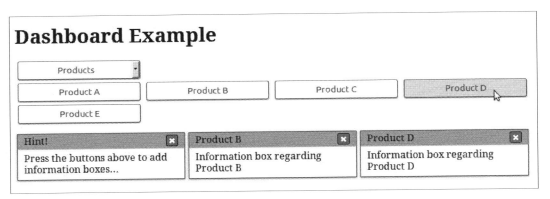

Our dashboard will initially contain a hint information box about the dashboard usage. Whenever a user clicks on one of the category items, a new information box will appear in our three-column layout dashboard. In the preceding image, the user has added two new information boxes for **Product B** and **Product D** by clicking on the associated buttons.

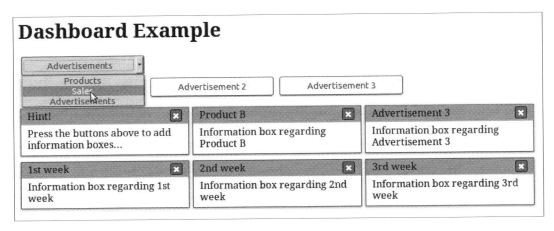

The user will also be able to dismiss any of these information boxes by clicking on a red close button on the top-right of each information box. In the preceding image, the user dismissed the **Product D** information box, then added information boxes for the **Advertisement 3** and later the 1st, 2nd, and 3rd week items of the **Sales** category.

By just reading the above description, we can easily isolate all the user interactions that are required for the implementation of our dashboard. We will need to add observers for each one of these user interactions and write code inside the callback functions that execute the appropriate DOM manipulations.

In detail, our code will need to:

- Observe changes done to the currently selected element and respond to such event by hiding or revealing the appropriate items
- Observe the clicks on each item button and respond by adding a new information box
- Observe the clicks on the close button of each information box and respond by removing it from the page

Now let's proceed and review the HTML, CSS, and JavaScript code required for the preceding example. Let's start with the HTML code and for reference, let's say that we saved it in a file named `Dashboard Example.html`, as follows:

```html
<!DOCTYPE html>
<html>
  <head>
    <title>Dashboard Example</title>
    <link rel="stylesheet" type="text/css"
        href="dashboard-example.css">
  </head>
  <body>
    <h1 id="pageHeader">Dashboard Example</h1>

    <div class="dashboardContainer">
      <section class="dashboardCategories">
        <select id="categoriesSelector">
          <option value="0" selected>Products</option>
          <option value="1">Sales</option>
          <option value="2">Advertisements</option>
        </select>
        <section class="dashboardCategory">
          <button>Product A</button>
          <button>Product B</button>
          <button>Product C</button>
```

```
        <button>Product D</button>
        <button>Product E</button>
      </section>
      <section class="dashboardCategory hidden">
        <button>1st week</button>
        <button>2nd week</button>
        <button>3rd week</button>
        <button>4th week</button>
      </section>
      <section class="dashboardCategory hidden">
        <button>Advertisement 1</button>
        <button>Advertisement 2</button>
        <button>Advertisement 3</button>
      </section>
      <div class="clear"></div>
    </section>

    <section class="boxContainer">
      <div class="boxsizer">
        <article class="box">
          <header class="boxHeader">
            Hint!
            <button class="boxCloseButton">&#10006;</button>
          </header>
          Press the buttons above to add information boxes...
        </article>
      </div>
    </section>
    <div class="clear"></div>
  </div>

  <script type="text/javascript" src="jquery.js"></script>
  <script type="text/javascript" src="dashboard-example.js">
  </script>
  </body>
</html>
```

In the preceding HTML, we placed all our dashboard-related elements inside a
`<div>` element with the `dashboardContainer` CSS class . This will enable us to have
a centric starting point to search for our dashboard's elements and also scope our
CSS. Inside it, we define two `<section>` elements in order to divide the dashboard
into logical areas using some HTML5 semantic elements.

The first `<section>` with the `dashboardCategories` class is used to hold the categories selector of our dashboard. Inside it, we have a `<select>` element with the ID `categoriesSelector` that is used to filter the visible category items and three subsections with the `dashboardCategory` class that are used to wrap the `<button>` elements that will populate the dashboard with information boxes when clicked. Two of them also have the `hidden` class so that only the first one is visible when the page loads by matching the initially selected option (`<option>`) of the category selector. Also, at the end of the first section, we also added a `<div>` with the `clear` class that, as we saw in the first chapter, will be used to clear the floated `<button>` elements.

The second `<section>` with the `boxContainer` class is used to hold the information boxes of our dashboard. Initially, it contains only one with a hint about how to use the dashboard. We use a `<div>` element with the `boxsizer` class to set the box dimensions and an HTML5 `<article>` element with the `box` class to add the required border padding and shadow, similar to the box elements from the first chapter.

Each information box, besides its content, also contains a `<header>` element with the `boxHeader` class and a `<button>` element with the `boxCloseButton` class that, when clicked, removes the information box that contains it. We also used the `&#10006;` HTML character code as the button's content in order to get a better-looking "x" mark and avoid using a separate image for that purpose.

Lastly, since the information boxes are also floated, we also need a `<div>` with the `clear` class at the end of the `boxContainer`.

In the `<head>` of the preceding HTML, we also reference a CSS file named as `dashboard-example.css` with the following content:

```css
.dashboardCategories {
    margin-bottom: 10px;
}

.dashboardCategories select,
.dashboardCategories button {
    display: block;
    width: 200px;
    padding: 5px 3px;
    border: 1px solid #333;
    margin: 3px 5px;
    border-radius: 3px;
    background-color: #FFF;
    text-align: center;
```

```css
    box-shadow: 0 1px 1px #777;
    cursor: pointer;
}

.dashboardCategories select:hover,
.dashboardCategories button:hover {
    background-color: #DDD;
}

.dashboardCategories button {
    float: left;
}

.box {
    padding: 7px 10px;
    border: solid 1px #333;
    margin: 5px 3px;
    box-shadow: 0 1px 2px #777;
}

.boxsizer {
    float: left;
    width: 33.33%;
}

.boxHeader {
    padding: 3px 10px;
    margin: -7px -10px 7px;
    background-color: #AAA;
    box-shadow: 0 1px 1px #999;
}

.boxCloseButton {
    float: right;
    height: 20px;
    width: 20px;
    padding: 0;
    border: 1px solid #000;
    border-radius: 3px;
    background-color: red;
    font-weight: bold;
    text-align: center;
    color: #FFF;
```

```
    cursor: pointer;
}


.clear { clear: both; }
.hidden { display: none; }
```

As you can see in our CSS file, first of all we add some space below the element with the `dashboardCategories` class and also define the same styling for the `<select>` element and the buttons inside it. In order to differentiate it from the default browser styling, we add some padding, a border with rounded corners, a different background color when hovering the mouse pointer, and some space in between them. We also define that our `<select>` element should be displayed alone in its row as a block and that the category item buttons should float next to each other. We again use the `boxsizer` and `box` CSS classes, as we did in *Chapter 1, A Refresher on jQuery and the Composite Pattern*; the first one to create a three-column layout and the second one to actually provide the styling of an information box. We continue by defining the `boxHeader` class that is applied to the `<header>` elements of our information boxes, and define some padding, a grey background color, a light shadow, and also some negative margins so that it counterbalances the effect of the box's paddings and places itself next to its border.

To complete the styling of the information boxes, we also define the `boxCloseButton` CSS class that (i) floats the box's close buttons to the upper-right corner inside the box `<header>`, (ii) defines a `20px` width and height, (iii) overrides the default browser's `<button>` styling to zero padding, and (iv) adds a single-pixel black border with rounded corners and a red background color. Lastly, like in *Chapter 1, A Refresher on jQuery and the Composite Pattern* we define the `clear` utility CSS class to prevent the element from being placed next to the previous floating elements and also define the `hidden` class as a convenient way of hiding elements of the page.

In our HTML file, we reference the jQuery library itself and also a JavaScript file named as `dashboard-example.js` that contains our dashboard implementation. Following the best practices of creating performant web pages, we have placed them right before the `</body>` tag, in order to avoid delaying the initial page rendering:

```
$(document).ready(function() {

    $('#categoriesSelector').change(function() {
        var $selector = $(this);
        var selectedIndex = +$selector.val();
        var $dashboardCategories = $('.dashboardCategory');
        var $selectedItem = $dashboardCategories.eq(selectedIndex)
            .show();
        $dashboardCategories.not($selectedItem).hide();
    });
```

```
function setupBoxCloseButton($box) {
    $box.find('.boxCloseButton').click(function() {
        $(this).closest('.boxsizer').remove();
    });
}

// make the close button of the hint box work
setupBoxCloseButton($('.box'));

$('.dashboardCategory button').on('click', function() {
    var $button = $(this);
    var boxHtml = '<div class="boxsizer"><article class="box">' +
        '<header class="boxHeader">' +
            $button.text() +
            '<button class="boxCloseButton">&#10006;' +
            '</button>' +
        '</header>' +
        'Information box regarding ' + $button.text() +
    '</article></div>';
    $('.boxContainer').append(boxHtml);
    setupBoxCloseButton($('.box:last-child'));
});

});
```

We have placed all our code inside a $(document).ready() call, in order to delay its execution until the DOM tree of the page is fully loaded. This would be absolutely required if we placed our code in the <head> element, but it is also a best practice that is good to follow in any case.

We first add an observer for the change event on the categoriesSelector element using the `$.fn.change()` method, which is actually a shorthand method for the $.fn.on('change', /* ... */) method. In jQuery, the value of the this keyword inside a function that is used as an observer holds a reference to the DOM element that the event was fired. This applies to all jQuery methods that register observers, from the core $.fn.on() to the $.fn.change() and $.fn.click() convenient methods. So we use the $() function to make a jQuery object with the <select> element and store it in the $selector variable. Then, we use $selector.val() to retrieve the value of the selected <option> and cast it to a numeric value by using the + operator. Right after this, we retrieve the <section> elements of dashboardCategory and cache the result to the $dashboardCategories variable. Then, we proceed by finding and revealing the category whose position is equal to the value of the selectedIndex variable and also store the resulting jQuery object to the $selectedItem variable. Finally, we are using the $selectedItem variable with the $.fn.not() method to retrieve and hide all the category elements, except from the one we just revealed.

In the next code section, we define the `setupBoxCloseButton` function that will be used to initialize the functionality of the close button. It expects a jQuery object with the box elements as a parameter, and for each of them, searches their descendants for the `boxCloseButton` CSS class that we use on the close buttons. Using `$.fn.click()`, which is a convenient method for `$.fn.on('click', /* fn */)`, we register an anonymous function to be executed whenever a click event is fired that uses the `$.fn.closest()` method to find the first ancestor element with the `boxsizer` class and removes it from the page. Right after this, we call this function once for the box elements that already existed in the page at the time when the page was loaded. In this case, the box element with the usage hint.

An extra thing to keep in mind when using the `$.fn.closest()` method is that it begins testing the given selector from the current element of the jQuery collection before proceeding with its ancestor elements. For more information, you can visit its documentation at `http://api.jquery.com/closest`.

In the final code section, we use the `$.fn.on()` method to add an observer for the click event on each of the category buttons. In this case, inside the anonymous observer function, we use the `this` keyword, which holds the DOM element of the `<button>` that was clicked, and use the `$()` method to create a jQuery object and cache its reference in the `$button` variable. Right after this, we retrieve the button's text content using the `$.fn.text()` method and along with it, construct the HTML code for the information box. For the close button, we use the `&#10006` HTML character code that will be rendered as a prettier "**X**" icon. The template we created is based on the HTML code of the initially visible hint box; for the needs of this chapter's example, we use plain string concatenation. Lastly, we append the generated HTML code for our box to the `boxContainer`, and since we expect it to be the last element, we use the `$()` function to find it and provide it as a parameter to the `setupBoxCloseButton`.

How it is compared with event attributes

Before the `EventTarget.addEventListener()` was defined in the DOM Level 2 Events specification, the event listeners were registered either by using the event attributes that are available for HTML elements or the element event properties that are available for DOM nodes.

For more information on the DOM Level 2 Event specification and event attributes, you can visit `http://www.w3.org/TR/DOM-Level-2-Events` and `https://developer.mozilla.org/en-US/docs/Web/Guide/HTML/Event_attributes`, respectively.

The event attributes are a set of attributes that are available to HTML elements and provide a declarative way of defining pieces of JavaScript code (preferably function calls) that should be executed when a specific event is triggered on that element. Because of their declarative nature and how simply they can be used, this is often the first way that new developers get introduced to events in web development.

If we used event attributes in the above example, then the HTML code for the close buttons in the information boxes will look as follows:

```
<article class="box">
    <header class="boxHeader">
        Hint!
        <button onclick="closeInfoBox();"
                class="boxCloseButton">&#10006;</button>
    </header>
    Press the buttons above to add information boxes...
</article>
```

Also, we should change the template that is used to create new information boxes and expose the `closeInfoBox` function on the `window` object, in order for it to be accessible from the HTML event attribute:

```
window.closeInfoBox = function() {
    $(this).closest('.boxsizer').remove();
};
```

Some of the disadvantages of using event attributes over the Observer Pattern are:

- It makes it harder to define multiple separate actions that have to be executed when an event fires on an element
- It makes the HTML code of the page bigger and less readable
- It is against the separation of concerns principle, since it adds JavaScript code inside our HTML, possibly making a bug harder to track and fix
- Most of the time, it leads to the functions being called in the event attribute getting exposed to the global `window` object, thereby "polluting" the global namespace

Using the element event properties would not require any changes to our HTML, keeping all the implementation in our JavaScript files. The changes required in our `setupBoxCloseButton` function will make it look as follows:

```
function setupBoxCloseButton($box) {
    var $closeButtons = $box.find('.boxCloseButton');
    for (var i = 0; i < $closeButtons.length; i++) {
        $closeButtons[i].onclick = function() {
            this.onclick = null;
            $(this).closest('.boxsizer').remove();
        };
    }
}
```

Note that, for convenience, we are still using jQuery for DOM manipulations, but the resulting code still has some of the aforementioned disadvantages. More importantly, in order to avoid memory leaks, we are also required to remove the function assigned to the `onclick` property before removing the element from the page, if it contains references to the DOM element that it is applied on.

Using the tools that today's browsers offer, we can even match the convenience that the declarative nature of event attributes offers. In the following image, you can see how the Firefox developer tools provide us with helpful feedback when we use them to inspect a page element that has an event listener attached:

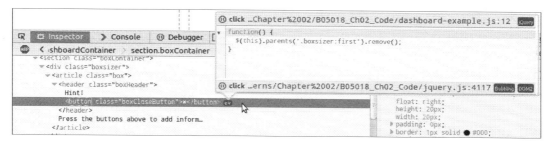

As you can see in the preceding image, all the elements that have observers attached also have an **ev** sign right next to them, which when clicked, displays a dialog showing all the event listeners that are currently attached. To make our developing experience even better, we can directly see the file and the line that these handlers were defined in. Moreover, we can click on them in order to expand and reveal their code, or click on the sign in front of them to navigate to their source and add breakpoints.

One of the biggest benefits of using the Observer Pattern over event attributes is clearly visible in the case where we need to take more than one action when a certain event happens. Suppose that we also need to add a new feature in our example dashboard, which would prevent a user from accidentally double-clicking a category item button and adding the same information box twice to the dashboard. The new implementation should ideally be completely independent from the existing one. Using the Observer Pattern, all we need to do is add the following code that observes for button clicks and disables that button for 700 milliseconds:

```
$(document).ready(function() {
  $('.dashboardCategory button').on('click', function() {
    var $button = $(this);
    $button.prop('disabled', true);

    setTimeout(function() {
      $button.prop('disabled', false);
    }, 700);
  });
});
```

The preceding code is indeed completely independent from the basic implementation and we could place it inside the same or a different JS file and load it to our page. This would be more difficult when using event attributes, since it would require us to define both actions at the same time inside the same event handler function; as a result, it would strongly couple the two independent actions.

Avoid memory leaks

As we saw earlier, there are some strong advantages of using the Observer Pattern to handle events on a web page. When using the `EventTarget.addEventListener()` method to add an observer to an element, we also need to keep in mind that in order to avoid memory leaks, we also have to call the `EventTarget.removeEventListener()` method before removing such elements from the page so that the observers are also removed.

 For more information on removing event listeners from elements, you can visit `https://developer.mozilla.org/en-US/docs/Web/API/EventTarget/removeEventListener`, or for the jQuery equivalent method, visit `http://api.jquery.com/off/`.

The jQuery library developers understood that such an implementation concern could easily be forgotten or not handled properly, thereby making the adoption of the Observer Pattern look more complex, so they decided to encapsulate the appropriate handling inside the `jQuery.event` implementation. As a result, when using any event handling jQuery method, such as the core `$.fn.on()` or any of the convenient methods such as `$.fn.click()` or `$.fn.change()`, the observer functions are tracked by jQuery itself and are properly unregistered if we later decide to remove the element from the page. As we saw earlier in the implementation of `jQuery.event`, jQuery stores a reference to the observers of each element in a separate mapping object. Every time we a use a jQuery method that removes DOM elements from the page, it first makes sure to remove any observers attached to those elements or any of the descendant elements, by checking the mapping object. As a result, the example code we used earlier is not causing memory leaks even though we are not using any method that explicitly removes the observers we add to the created elements.

Be careful when mixing jQuery and plain DOM manipulations

Even though all jQuery methods keep you safe from memory leaks caused from observers that are never unregistered, keep in mind it can't protect you if you remove elements using plain methods from the DOM API. If methods such as `Element.remove()` and `Element.removeChild()` are used and the removed elements or their descendants have observers attached, then they are not going to be unregistered automatically. The same applies when assigning to the `Element.innerHTML` property.

Introducing the Delegated Event Observer Pattern

Now that we have learned some advanced details about how to use the Observer Pattern using jQuery, we will get introduced to a special variation of it that fits perfectly to the web platform and provides some extra benefits. The Delegated Event Observer Pattern (or simply Delegate Observer Pattern) is often used in web development and it utilizes the bubbling feature that most events that are fired on DOM elements have. For example, when we click on a page element, the click event is immediately fired on it, and right after this it also fires on all its parent elements until it reaches the root of our HTML document. Using a slightly different overloaded version of the jQuery's `$.fn.on` method, we can easily create and attach observers on page elements for delegated events that are fired on specific child elements.

The term "Event Delegation" describes the programming pattern where the handler of an event is not attached directly to the element of interest, but is instead attached to one of its ancestor elements.

How it simplifies our code

Reimplementing our dashboard example using the Delegated Event Observer Pattern will require us to change only the code of the included JavaScript file to the following:

```javascript
$(document).ready(function() {

    $('#categoriesSelector').change(function() {
        var $selector = $(this);
        var selectedIndex = +$selector.val();
        var $dashboardCategories = $('.dashboardCategory');
        var $selectedItem = $dashboardCategories.eq(selectedIndex)
            .show();
        $dashboardCategories.not($selectedItem).hide();
    });

    $('.dashboardCategories').on('click', 'button', function() {
        var $button = $(this);
        var boxHtml = '<div class="boxsizer"><article class="box">' +
                '<header class="boxHeader">' +
                    $button.text() +
                    '<button class="boxCloseButton">&#10006;' +
                    '</button>' +
                '</header>' +
                'Information box regarding ' + $button.text() +
            '</article></div>';
        $('.boxContainer').append(boxHtml);
    });

    $('.boxContainer').on('click', '.boxCloseButton', function() {
        $(this).closest('.boxsizer').remove();
    });

});
```

The most obvious difference is that the new implementation is shorter. The benefits come by defining just one observer to a common ancestor element, for each action that applies to more than one page element. For this reason, we use the `$.fn.on(events, selector, handler)` overload variation of the `$.fn.on()` method.

Specifically, we add an observer to the page element with the `dashboardCategories` CSS class and listen for the `click` events that originate from any of its `<button>` descendants. Similarly, we add a single observer to the `boxContainer` element that will be executed whenever a click event fires on any of its descendants that match the `.boxCloseButton` CSS selector.

Since the above observers apply not only to the elements that existed in the page at the moment they were registered, but also to any element that is added at any later point of time and matches the specified CSS selector; we are able to decouple the code that handles the clicks on the close buttons and place it in a separate observer, instead of registering a new one every time a new information box is added. As a result, the observer that adds the new information boxes in the dashboard is simpler and only has to deal with creating the HTML of the box and insert it into the dashboard, leading to a greater separation of concerns. Moreover, we no longer need to handle the registration of the observer for the close button of the hint box in a separate piece of code.

Compare the memory usage benefits

We will now compare the difference in memory usage when using the `$.fn.on()` method with the simple and Delegated Event Observer Pattern variation. To achieve this we will open the two implementations of our dashboard example and compare their memory usage on Chrome. To open Chrome's developer tools, just press *F12* and then navigate to the **Timeline** tab. We press the "record" button in the Chrome's **Timeline** tab and then press each category item button 10 times, resulting in the addition of 120 information boxes to our dashboard. After adding all the boxes, we end up with 121 open boxes in total, since the hint box will still be open and then stop the timeline recording.

The results in the timeline for our initial Observer Pattern implementation will look as follows:

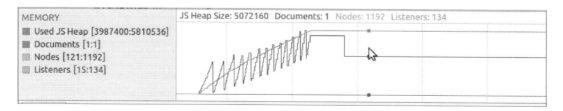

Repeating the same process for the Delegated Event Observer Pattern implementation will give a smoother timeline, revealing less object allocations and Garbage Collections, as follows:

As you can see in the preceding images, we end up with 1192 page elements in both cases, but in the first implementation we are using 134 event listeners, as compared to the implementation with event delegation where we initially created three event listeners and never actually added another.

Finally, as you can see from the blue line in the graph, the memory consumption of the delegate version stayed relatively the same, adding up to just around 200 KB. On the other hand, in the original implementation, the heap size increased more than five times, gaining more than 1 MB of increase.

Adding so many elements may not be an actual use case, but the dashboard will probably not be the only dynamic part of your page. As a result, in a relatively complex web page, we could get similar improvements if we reimplemented every applicable part of it using the Delegated Event Observer Pattern variant.

Summary

In this chapter, we learned about the Observer Pattern, how it can make the HTML code of our web pages cleaner, and the way that decouples it from our application's code. We learned how jQuery adds a protection layer to its methods in order to protect us from undetected memory leaks, which may occur by adding observers to elements, when not using the jQuery DOM manipulation methods.

We also tried the Delegated Event Observer Pattern variant and used it to rewrite our initial example. We compared the two implementations and saw how it simplifies writing code that applies to many page elements when they are generated after the page has been loaded. Finally, we had a comparison regarding the memory consumption of the plain Observer Pattern with its delegate variant and highlighted how it also lessens the memory consumption of our page by reducing the required number of attached observers.

Now that we have completed our introduction on how the Observer Pattern is used to listen to user actions, we can move on to the next chapter where we will learn about custom events and the Publish/Subscribe Pattern and the way they can lead to a more decoupled implementation.

3
The Publish/Subscribe Pattern

In this chapter, we will showcase the Publish/Subscribe Pattern, a design pattern quite similar to the Observer Pattern but with a more distinct role that is a better fit for more complex use cases. We will see how it differs from the Observer Pattern and how jQuery adopted some of its concepts and brought them to its Observer Pattern implementation.

Later, we will proceed and rewrite our previous chapter's example using this pattern. We will use this pattern's benefits to add some extra features and also reduce the coupling of our code with the elements of the web page.

In this chapter, we will:

- Introduce the Publish/Subscribe Pattern
- Learn how it differs and what advantages it has over the Observer Pattern
- Learn how jQuery brings some of its features to its methods
- Learn how to emit custom events with jQuery
- Rewrite and extend the example from *Chapter 2, The Observer Pattern,* using this pattern

Introducing the Publish/Subscribe Pattern

The Publish/Subscribe Pattern is a Messaging Pattern where the emitters of the messages, called the **publishers**, multicast messages to a number of recipients, called the **subscribers**, that have expressed their interest in receiving such messages. The key concept of this pattern, which is also commonly referred to as the Pub/Sub Pattern in short, is to provide a way to avoid dependencies between the publishers and their subscribers.

An extra concept of this pattern is the use of **topics** that are used by the subscribers in order to express that they are only interested in messages of a specific type. This way, publishers filter subscribers before sending a message and distribute that message only to the appropriate ones, thereby reducing the amount of traffic and work required on both sides.

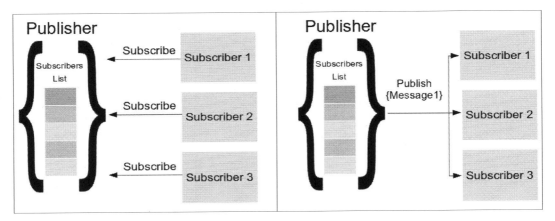

Another common variant is to use a central, application-wide object, known as the **broker**, that relays messages produced by the publishers to the relevant subscribers. The broker, in this case, acts as a well-known message handler to send and subscribe to message topics. This enables us, instead of coupling different application parts together, to only reference the broker itself and also the topic that our components are interested in. Even though topics might not be an absolute requirement in the first variant of this pattern, this variant plays an essential role in scalability since there will commonly exist way less brokers (if not just one) than publishers and subscribers.

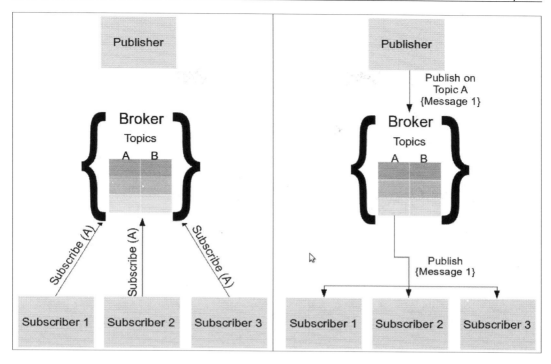

By following a subscription scheme, the code of the publisher is completely decoupled from the subscribers, meaning that the publisher does not have to know the objects depend on them. As a result, we do not need to hard code to the publisher each separate action that should be executed on the different parts of our application. Instead, the components of an application, and possibly third-party extensions, subscribe to be notified only about topics/events that they need to know. In such distributed architecture, adding a new feature to an existing application requires minimal to no changes to the application components it depends on.

How it differs from the Observer Pattern

The most basic difference is that, by definition, the Pub/Sub Pattern is a one-way-Messaging Pattern that can also pass a message, unlike the Observer Pattern that just describes how to notify the observers about a specific state change on the subject.

Moreover, unlike the Observer Pattern, the Pub/Sub Pattern with a broker results in more loosely coupled code for the different parts of an implementation. This is because the observers need to know their subject that is emitting the events; however, on the other hand, the publishers and their subscribers only need to know the broker that is used.

How it is adopted by jQuery

Once again, the jQuery library provides us with a convenient way to take advantage of the Pub/Sub Pattern in our code. Instead of extending its API by adding new methods specifically named "publish" and "subscribe" and introducing new concepts, the developers decided to extend the `jQuery.fn.on()` and `jQuery.fn.trigger()` methods with the ability to handle and emit custom events. This way, jQuery can be used to implement a publisher/subscriber communication scheme using the already known convenient methods it provides.

Custom events in jQuery

Custom events allow us to use almost any user-defined string value as a common event that we can add listeners for, and also manually fire it on page elements. As an extra but a precious feature, custom events can also carry some extra data to be delivered to the listeners of the event.

The jQuery library added its own custom events implementation, before it was actually added to any web specification. This way, it was proved how useful they can be when used in web development. As we saw in the previous chapter, in jQuery, there is a specific part of the implementation that handles both the common element event and also custom events. The `jQuery.event` object holds all the internal implementations related to firing and listening to events. Also, the `jQuery.Event` class is a dedicated wrapper that jQuery uses for the needs of both the common element events and its custom events implementation.

Implementing a Pub/Sub scheme using custom events

In the previous chapter, we saw how the `jQuery.fn.on()` method can be used to add event listeners on elements. We also saw that its implementation is maintaining lists with the added handlers and notifying them when required. Moreover, the event name seems to have the same coordination purpose, just like the topic. This implementation semantics seem to match exactly with the Pub/Sub Pattern as well.

The `jQuery.fn.trigger()` method actually uses the internal `jQuery.event.trigger()` method that is used to fire events in jQuery. It iterates over the internal handlers list and executes them with the requested event along with any extra parameters that the custom event defines. Once again, this also matches the operation requirements of the Pub/Sub Pattern.

As a result, `jQuery.fn.trigger()` and `jQuery.fn.on()` seem to match the needs of the Pub/Sub Pattern and can be used instead of separate "publish" and "subscribe" methods, respectively. Since they are both available on the `jQuery.fn` object, we can use these methods on any jQuery object. This jQuery object will act as an intermediate entity between the publishers and the subscribers, in a way that perfectly aligns with the definition of the broker.

A good common practice, which is also used by a lot of jQuery plugins, is to use the outermost page element that holds the implementation of the application or the plugin as the broker. On the other hand, jQuery actually allows us to use any object as a broker, since all that it actually needs is a target to emit an observe for our custom events. As a result, we could even use an empty object as our broker such as `$({})`, in case using a page element seems too restricting or not clean enough according to the Pub/Sub Pattern. This is actually what the jQuery Tiny Pub/Sub library does, along with some method aliasing, so that we actually use methods named "publish" and "subscribe" instead of jQuery's "on" and "trigger". For more information on Tiny, you can visit its repository page at `https://github.com/cowboy/jquery-tiny-pubsub`.

Demonstrating a sample use case

In order to see how the Pub/Sub Pattern is used, and make it easy to compare it with the Observer Pattern, we are going to rewrite the dashboard example from *Chapter 2, The Observer Pattern*, using this pattern. This will also clearly demonstrate how this pattern can help us decouple the individual parts of an implementation and make it more extendable and scalable.

Using Pub/Sub on the dashboard example

For the needs of this demonstration, we will use the HTML and CSS files exactly as we saw them in *Chapter 2, The Observer Pattern*.

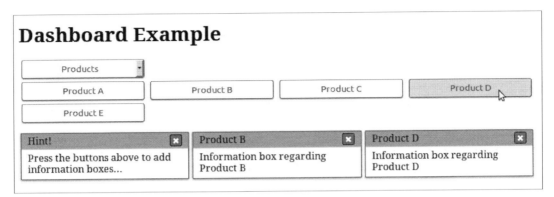

To apply this pattern, we will only need to change the code in the JavaScript file with our new implementation. In the following code snippet, we can see how the code was changed in order to adapt to the Publisher/Subscriber Pattern:

```
$(document).ready(function() {
    window.broker = $('.dashboardContainer');

    $('#categoriesSelector').change(function() {
        var $selector = $(this);
        var message = { categoryID: $selector.val() };
        broker.trigger('dashboardCategorySelect', [message]);
    });

    broker.on('dashboardCategorySelect', function(event, message) {
        var $dashboardCategories = $('.dashboardCategory');
        var selectedIndex = +message.categoryID;
        var $selectedItem = $dashboardCategories.eq(selectedIndex)
            .show();
        $dashboardCategories.not($selectedItem).hide();
    });

    $('.dashboardCategory').on('click', 'button', function() {
        var $button = $(this);
        var message = { categoryName: $button.text() };
        broker.trigger('categoryItemOpen', [message]);
    });
```

```
broker.on('categoryItemOpen', function(event, message) {
    var boxHtml = '<div class="boxsizer"><article class="box">' +
        '<header class="boxHeader">' +
            message.categoryName +
            '<button class="boxCloseButton">&#10006;' +
            '</button>' +
        '</header>' +
        'Information box regarding ' + message.categoryName +
        '</article></div>';
    $('.boxContainer').append(boxHtml);
});

$('.boxContainer').on('click', '.boxCloseButton', function() {
    var boxIndex = $(this).closest('.boxsizer').index();
    var message = { boxIndex: boxIndex };
    broker.trigger('categoryItemClose', [message]);
});

broker.on('categoryItemClose', function(event, message) {
    $('.boxContainer .boxsizer').eq(message.boxIndex).remove();
});
});
```

Just like in our previous implementation, we use $(document).ready() in order to delay the execution of our code until the page has been fully loaded. First of all, we declare our broker and assign it to a new variable on the window object so that it is globally available on the page. For our application's broker, we are using a jQuery object with the outermost container of our implementation, which in our case is the <div> element with the dashboardContainer class.

Even though using global variables is generally an anti-pattern, we store the broker into a global variable since it is an important synchronization point of the whole application and must be available for every piece of our implementation, even to those that are stored in separate .js files. As we will discuss in the next chapter about the Module Pattern, the preceding code could be improved by storing the broker as a property of the application's namespace.

In order to implement the category selector, we are first observing the `<select>` element for the `change` event. When the selected category changes, we create our message using a plain JavaScript object with the `value` of the selected `<option>` stored in the `categoryID` property. Then, we publish it in the `dashboardCategorySelect` topic using the jQuery `jQuery.fn.trigger()` method on our broker. This way, we move from a UI element event to a message with application semantics that contains all the required information. Right below, in our subscriber's code, we are using the `jQuery.fn.on()` method on our broker with the `dashboardCategorySelect` topic as a parameter (our custom event), just like we would do to listen for a simple DOM event. The subscriber then uses the `categoryID` from the received message, just like we did in the implementation of the previous chapter, to display the appropriate category items.

Following the same approach, we split the code that handles adding and closing information boxes in our dashboard in publishers and subscribers. For the needs of this demonstration, the message of the `categoryItemOpen` topic contains just the name of the category we want to open. However, in an application where the box content is retrieved from a server, we would probably use a category item ID instead. The subscriber then uses the category item name from the message to create and insert the requested information box.

Similarly, the message for the `categoryItemClose` topic contains the index of the box that we want removed. Our publisher uses the `jQuery.fn.closest()` method to traverse the DOM and reach the child elements of our `boxContainer` element and then uses the `jQuery.fn.index()` method to find its position among its siblings. The subscriber then uses `jQuery.fn.eq()` and the `boxIndex` property from the received message to filter and remove only the requested information box from the dashboard.

In a more complex application, instead of the box index, we can associate each information box element with a newly retrieved `jQuery.guid` using a mapping object. This will allow our publisher to use that `guid` in the message instead of the (DOM-related) element index. The subscriber will then search the mapping object for that `guid` in order to locate and remove the appropriate box.

Since we are trying to demonstrate the advantages of the Pub/Sub Pattern, this implementation change was not introduced in order to ease the comparison with the Observer Pattern and is instead left as a recommended exercise for the reader.

To summarize the above, we used the `dashboardCategorySelect`, `categoryItemOpen`, and `categoryItemClose` topics as our application-level events in order to decouple the handling of the user actions from their origin (the UI element). As a result, we now have dedicated reusable pieces of code that manipulate our dashboard's content, which is equivalent to abstracting them into separate functions. This allows us to programmatically publish a series of messages so that we can, for example, remove all the existing information boxes and add all the category items of the currently selected category. Alternatively, even better, make the dashboard show all the items of each category for 10 seconds and then move to the next one.

Extending the implementation

In order to demonstrate the scalability that the Pub/Sub Pattern brings with it, we will extend our current example by adding a counter with the number of boxes that are currently open in the dashboard.

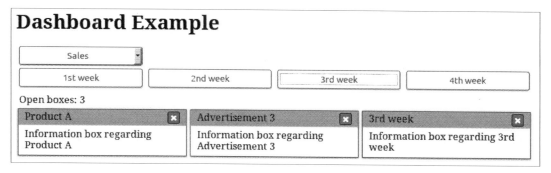

For the counter implementation, we will need to add some extra HTML to our page and also create and reference a new JavaScript file to hold the counter implementation:

```
...
</section>
<div style="margin-left: 5px;">
  Open boxes:
  <output id="dashboardItemCounter">1</output>
</div>
<section class="boxContainer">
...
```

In the HTML page of the example, we will need to add an extra `<div>` element to hold our counter and some description text. For our counter, we are using an `<output>` element, which is a semantic HTML5 element ideal to present results of user actions. The browser will use it just like a normal `<span>` element, so it will appear right next to its description. Also, since there is initially a hint box open in our dashboard, we use a 1 for its initial content:

```
$(document).ready(function() {
    broker.on('categoryItemOpen categoryItemClose',
        function (event, message) {
        var $counter = $('#dashboardItemCounter');
        var count = parseInt($counter.text());

        if (event.type === 'categoryItemOpen') {
            $counter.text(count + 1);
        } else if (event.type === 'categoryItemClose' && count > 0) {
            $counter.text(count - 1);
        }
    });
});
```

For the counter implementation itself, all we need to do is add an extra subscriber to the dashboard's broker, which is globally available to other JavaScript files loaded in the page, since we have attached it to the `window` object. We are simultaneously subscribing to two topics, by passing them space delimited to the `jQuery.fn.on()` method. Right after this, we locate the counter `<output>` element that has the ID `dashboardItemCounter` and parse its text content as a number. In order to differentiate our action, based on the topic that the message has received, we use the `event` object that jQuery passes as the first parameter to our anonymous function, which is our subscriber. Specifically, we use the `type` property of the `event` object that holds the topic name of the message that was received and based on its value, we change the content of the counter.

 For more information on the event object that jQuery provides, you can visit `http://api.jquery.com/category/events/event-object/`.

Similarly, we could also rewrite the code that prevents accidental double-clicks on the category item buttons. All that is needed is to add an extra subscriber for the `categoryItemOpen` topic and use the `categoryName` property of the message to locate the pressed button.

Using any object as a broker

While in our example we used the outermost container element of our dashboard for our broker, it is also common to use the $(document) object as a broker. Using the application's container element is considered a good semantic practice, which also scopes the emitted events.

As we described earlier in this chapter, jQuery actually allows us to use any object as a broker, even an empty one. As a result, we could instead use something such as window.broker = $({}); for our broker, in case we prefer it over using a page element.

By using newly constructed empty objects, we can also easily create several brokers, in case such a thing would be preferred for a specific implementation. Moreover, in case a centralized broker is not preferred, we could just make each publisher the broker of itself, leading to an implementation more like the first/basic variant of the Pub/Sub Pattern.

Since in most cases, a declared variable is used to access the application's broker within a page, there is little difference between the above approaches. Just choose the one that better matches your team's taste, and in case you change your mind at a later point, all you have to do is use a different assignment on your broker variable.

Using custom event namespacing

As a closing note for this chapter, we will present, in short, the mechanism that jQuery provides for namespacing custom events. The main benefit of event namespacing is that it allows us to use more specific event names that better describe their purpose, while also helping us to avoid conflicts between different implementation parts and plugins. It also provides a convenient way to unbind all the events of a given namespace from any target (element or broker).

A simple example implementation will look as follows:

```
var broker = $({});
broker.on('close.dialog', function (event, message){
    console.log(event.type, event.namespace);
});
broker.trigger('close.dialog', ['messageEmitted']);
broker.off('.dialog');
// removes all event handlers of the "dialog" namespace
```

For more information, you can visit the documentation page at `http://docs.jquery.com/Namespaced_Events` and the article at `https://css-tricks.com/namespaced-events-jquery/` from the CSS-Tricks website.

Summary

In this chapter, we were introduced to the Publish/Subscribe Pattern. We saw its similarities with the Observer Pattern and also learned its benefits by doing a comparison of the two. We analyzed how the more distinct roles and the extra features that the Publish/Subscribe Pattern offers make it an ideal pattern for more complex use cases. We saw how jQuery developers adopted some of its concepts and brought them to their Observer Pattern implementation as custom events. Finally, we rewrote the example from the previous chapter using the Publish/Subscribe Pattern, adding some extra features and also achieving greater decoupling between the different parts and page elements of our application.

Now that we have completed our introduction to how the Publish/Subscribe Pattern can be used as a first step to decouple the different parts of an implementation, we can move on to the next chapter where we will be introduced to the Module Pattern. In the next chapter, we will learn how to separate the different parts of an implementation into independent modules and how to use namespacing to achieve better code organization and define a strict API to achieve communication between the different modules.

4
Divide and Conquer with the Module Pattern

In this chapter, we will be introduced to the concepts of Modules and Namespacing and see how they can lead to more robust implementations. We will showcase how these design principles can be used in applications, by demonstrating some of the most commonly used development patterns to create **Modules** in JavaScript.

In this chapter, we will:

- Review the concept of Modules and Namespacing
- Introduce the Object Literal Pattern
- Introduce the Module Pattern and its variants
- Introduce the Revealing Module Pattern and its variants
- Have a small dive into ES5 Strict Mode and ES6 Modules
- Explain how Modules can be used and benefit jQuery applications

Modules and Namespaces

The two main practices of this chapter are Modules and Namespaces, which are used together in order to structure and organize our code. We will first analyze the main concept of Modules that is code encapsulation and right after this, we will proceed to Namespacing, which is used to logically organize an implementation.

Encapsulating internal parts of an implementation

While developing a large-scale and complex web application, the need for a well-defined, structured architecture becomes clear from the beginning. In order to avoid creating a spaghetti code implementation, where different parts of our code call each other in a chaotic way, we have to split our application into small, self-contained parts.

These self-contained pieces of code can be defined as **Modules**. To document this architecture principle, **Computer Science** has defined concepts such as **Separation of Concerns**, where the role, operation, and the exposed API of each Module should be strictly defined and focused on providing a generic solution to a specific problem.

 For more information on **Encapsulation** and **Separation of Concerns**, you can visit https://developer.mozilla.org/en-US/docs/Glossary/Encapsulation and http://aspiringcraftsman.com/2008/01/03/art-of-separation-of-concerns/.

Avoiding global variables with Namespaces

In JavaScript, the window object is also known as the **Global Namespace**, where each declared variable and function identifier is attached by default. A **Namespace** can be defined as a naming context where each identifier has to be unique. The main concept of **Namespacing** is to provide a way to logically group all the related pieces of a distinct and self-contained part of an application. In other words, it suggests that we create groups with related functions and variables and make them accessible under the same umbrella identifier. This helps to avoid naming collisions between different parts of an application and other JavaScript libraries that are used, since we only need to keep all the identifiers unique under each different Namespace.

A good example of Namespacing is the mathematical functions and constants that JavaScript provides, which are grouped under the built-in JavaScript object called Math. Since JavaScript provides more than 40 short-named mathematical identifiers, such as E, PI, and floor(), in order to avoid naming conflicts and grouping them together, it was designed to make them accessible as properties of the Math object that acts as the Namespace of this built-in library.

Without proper Namespacing, each function and variable needs to be uniquely named through the entire application, and collisions could happen between the identifiers of different application parts or even with those of a third-party library that an application uses. Finally, while Modules provide a way to isolate each independent part of your application, Namespacing provides a way to structure your different Modules to what becomes the architecture of the application.

The benefits of these patterns

Designing an application architecture based on Modules and namespacing leads to better code organization and clearly separated parts. In such architectures, Modules are used to group together parts of the implementation that are related, while Namespaces connect them to each other to create the application structure.

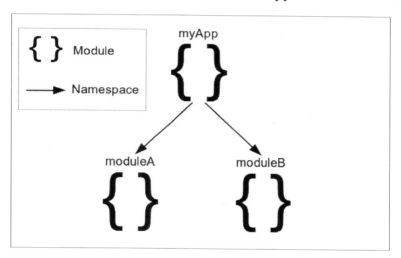

This architecture helps to coordinate large developer teams, enabling the implementation of independent parts to take place in parallel. It can also shorten the development time needed to add a new functionality to the existing implementation. This is because the existing pieces that are used can be located easily and the added implementation has less chance of conflicting with the existing code.

The resulting code structures are not only cleanly separated, but since each Module is designed to achieve a single goal, there is a good chance that it can also be used in other similar applications. As an added benefit, since the role of each Module is strictly defined, it also makes tracing the origin of a bug a lot easier in a large codebase.

The wide acceptance

Both the community and the enterprise world realized that, in order to have maintainable, large frontend applications written in JavaScript, they should end up with a set of best practices that should be incorporated in every part of their implementations.

The acceptance and adoption of Modules and Namespacing in JavaScript implementations is clearly visible in the best practices and coding style guides that the community and enterprises have released.

For example, Google's JavaScript Style Guide (available at `https://google.github.io/styleguide/javascriptguide.xml#Naming`) describes and suggests adopting namespacing in our implementations:

> *ALWAYS prefix identifiers in the global scope with a unique pseudo namespace related to the project or library.*

Moreover, the jQuery JavaScript Style Guide (available at `https://contribute.jquery.org/style-guide/js/#global-variables`) suggests using global variables so that:

> *Each project may expose at most one global variable.*

Another example of acceptance among the developer community, comes from the Mozilla Developer Network. Its guide for object-oriented JavaScript (available at `https://developer.mozilla.org/en-US/docs/Web/JavaScript/Introduction_to_Object-Oriented_JavaScript#Namespace`) also suggests using Namespaces, to wrap the implementation of our application under a single exposed variable, using something as simple as follows:

```
// global namespace
var MYAPP = MYAPP || {};
```

The Object Literal Pattern

The Object Literal Pattern is probably the simplest way to wrap all the related parts of an implementation under an umbrella object that works as a Module. The name of this pattern accurately describes the way it is used. The developer just needs to declare a variable and assign an object with all the related parts that need to be encapsulated into this Module.

Let's see how we can create a Module that provides unique integers to a page, in a similar way how `jquery.guid` does it:

```
var simpleguid = {
  guid: 1,
  init: function() {
    this.guid = 1;
  },
  increaseCounter: function() {
    this.guid++;
    // or simpleguid.guid++;
  },
  getNext: function() {
    var nextGuid = this.guid;
    this.increaseCounter();
    return nextGuid;
  }
};
```

As seen above, a simple rule that you can follow in order to adopt this pattern is to define all the variables and functions that each implementation needs as properties of an object. Our code is reusable and does not pollute the Global Namespace, other than just defining a single variable name for our Module, `simpleguid` in this case.

We can access the Module properties internally, either by using the `this` keyword, such as `this.guid`, or using the full name of the Module such as `simpleguid.guid`. In order to use the above Module in our code, we just need to access its property by using its name. For example, calling the `simpleguid.getNext()` method will return to our code the next-in-order numeric guid and also change the Module's state by increasing the internal counter.

One of the negatives of this pattern is that it does not provide any privacy to the internal parts of the Module. All the internal parts of the Module can be accessed and be overridden by external code, even though we ideally prefer to only expose the `simpleguid.init()` and `simpleguid.getNext()` methods. There are several naming conventions that describe prepending or appending an underscore (_) to the names of properties that are intended only for internal use, but this technically doesn't fix this disadvantage.

Another disadvantage is that writing a big Module using an object literal can easily get tiring. It's true that JavaScript developers are used to end their variables and function definitions with semicolons (;), and trying to write a big Module using commas (,) after each property can easily lead to syntactic errors.

Even though this pattern makes it easy to declare nested Namespaces for a Module, it can also lead to big code structures with bad readability in case we need several levels of nesting. For example, let's take a look at the following skeleton of a Todo application:

```
var myTodoApp = {
  todos: [],
  addTodo: function(todo) { this.todos.push(todo); },
  getTodos: function() { return this.todos; },
  updateTodo: function(todo) { /*...*/ },
  imports: {
    fromGDrive: function() { /*...*/ },
    fromUrl: function() { /*...*/ },
    fromText: function() { /*...*/ }
  },
  exports: {
    gDrivePublicKey: '#wnanqAASnsmkkw',
    toGDrive: function() { /*...*/ },
    toFile: function() { /*...*/ },
  },
  share: {
    toTwitter: function(todo) { /*...*/ }
  }
};
```

Fortunately, this can be easily fixed by splitting the object literal to multiple assignments for each submodule (and preferably to different files) as follows:

```
var myTodoApp = {
  todos: [],
  addTodo: function(todo) { this.todos.push(todo); },
  getTodos: function() { return this.todos; },
  updateTodo: function(todo) { /*...*/ },
};
/* … */
myTodoApp.exports = {
  gDrivePublicKey: '#wnanqAASnsmkkw',
  toGDrive: function() { /*...*/ },
  toFile: function() { /*...*/ },
};
/*...*/
```

The Module Pattern

The key concept of the basic Module Pattern is to provide a simple function, class, or object that the rest of the application can use, through a well-known variable name. It enables us to provide a minimal API for a Module, by hiding the parts of the implementation that do not need to be exposed. This way, we also avoid polluting the Global Namespace with variables and utility functions that are needed for internal use by our Module.

The IIFE building block

In this subsection, we will get a small introduction to the IIFE Design Pattern since it's an integral part for all the variants of the Module Pattern that we will see in this chapter. The **Immediately Invoked Function Expression (IIFE)** is a very commonly used Design Pattern among JavaScript developers because of the clean way in which it isolates blocks of code. In the Module Pattern, an IIFE is used to wrap all the implementation in order to avoid polluting the Global Namespace and provide privacy to the declarations to the Module itself.

Each IIFE creates a Closure with the variables and functions declared inside it. The Closure that is created enables the exposed function of the IIFE to keep references to the rest of the declarations of their environment and access them normally when executed from other parts of an implementation. As a result, the non-exposed declarations of the IIFE do not leak outside it, but are kept private and are accessible only by the functions that are part of the created Closure.

 For more information on IIFEs and Closures, you can visit `https://developer.mozilla.org/en-US/docs/Glossary/IIFE` and `https://developer.mozilla.org/en-US/docs/Web/JavaScript/Closures`.

An IIFE is most commonly used as follows:

```
(function() {
  var x = 7;
  console.log(x);
  // prints 7
})();
```

Since the preceding code construct might look bizarre on first sight, let's see the pieces that it is composed from. An IIFE is almost equivalent to declaring an anonymous function, assigning it to a variable, and then executing it, as shown in the following code:

```
var tmp = function() {
  var x = 7;
  console.log(x);
};

tmp();
// or
(tmp)();
```

In the preceding code, we define a function expression and execute it using `tmp()`. Since, in JavaScript, we can use parentheses around an identifier without changing its meaning, we can also execute the stored function with `(tmp)();`. The final step, in order to turn the preceding code into an IIFE, is to replace the `tmp` variable with the actual anonymous function declaration.

As we saw earlier, the only difference is that, with an IIFE, we do need to declare a variable just to hold the function itself. We only create an anonymous function and invoke it immediately right after defining it.

Since the creation of an IIFE can be achieved in several ways, which might look like an exercise of JavaScript's rules, the community of JavaScript developers has concluded to the above code structure as a point of reference for this pattern. This way of creating an IIFE is considered to have better readability and is used by large libraries and as a result of its adoption, developers can easily recognize it inside large JavaScript implementations.

An example of the less-widely-used ways to create an IIFE is the following code structure:

```
(function() {
  // code
}());
```

The simple IIFE Module Pattern

Since there is no actual name for this pattern, it is recognized by the fact that the defined Module returns a single entity. For reference on how to create a reusable library using this pattern, we will rewrite the `simpleguid` Module that we saw earlier. The resulting implementation will look as follows:

```
var simpleguid = (function() {
  var simpleguid = {};
  var guid;

  simpleguid.init = function() {
    guid = 1;
  };

  simpleguid.increaseCounter = function() {
    guid++;
  };

  simpleguid.getNext = function() {
    var nextGuid = guid;
    this.increaseCounter();
    return nextGuid;
  };

  simpleguid.init();

  return simpleguid;
})();
```

This pattern uses an IIFE to define an object that acts as the Module container, attaches properties to it, and later returns it. The variable `simpleguid` in the first line of the preceding code is used as the Namespace of the Module and is assigned with the value that is returned by the IIFE. The methods and properties that are defined on the returned object are the only exposed parts of the Modules and constitute its public API.

Once again, this pattern allows us to use the `this` keyword, in order to access the exposed methods and properties of our Module. Furthermore, it also provides the flexibility to execute any required initialization code before completing the Module's definition.

Unlike the **Object Literal Pattern**, the **Module Pattern** enables us to create actual private members in our Modules. Variables declared inside the IIFE, that are not attached to the return value, such as the guid variable, act as private members and are only accessible inside the Module by rest members of the created Closure.

Lastly, in case we need to define a nested Namespace, all we have to do is change the assignment of the value returned by the IIFE. As an example of an application structured with submodules, let's see how we will define the exporting submodule for the Todo application skeleton that we saw earlier:

```
var myTodoApp = (function() {
  var myTodoApp = {};

  var todos = [];

  myTodoApp.addTodo = function(todo) {
    todos.push(todo);
  };

  myTodoApp.getTodos = function() {
    return todos;
  };

  return myTodoApp;
})();

myTodoApp.exports = (function() {
  var exports = {};

  var gDrivePublicKey = '#wnanqAASnsmkkw';

  exports.toGDrive = function() { /*...*/ };

  exports.toFile = function() { /*...*/ };

  return exports;
})();
```

Given that our application's Namespace myTodoApp has already been defined earlier, the exports submodule can be defined as a simple property on it. A good practice to follow will be to create one file for each one of the above Modules, using the IIFEs as the landmarks to split your code. A widely used naming convention, which is also suggested by Google's JavaScript Style Guide, is to use lowercase naming for your files and add dashes to separate submodules. For example, by following this naming convention, the preceding code should be defined in two files named as mytodoapp.js and mytodoapp-exports.js for each Module, respectively.

How it is used by jQuery

The **Module Pattern** is used within jQuery itself, in order to isolate the source code of the CSS selector engine (**Sizzle**), which powers the `$()` function, from the rest of the jQuery source. From the beginning, Sizzle was a big part of the jQuery source, which is currently counting about 2135 lines of code; since 2009, it has been split into a separate project named Sizzle, so it can be more easily maintained, be developed independently, and be reusable by other libraries:

```
var Sizzle = (function(window) {

  /* 179 lines of code */

  function Sizzle(selector, context, results, seed) {
    /* 131 lines of code */
  }

  /*
    1804 lines of code , defining methods like:
    Sizzle.attr
    Sizzle.compile
    Sizzle.contains
    Sizzle.getText
    Sizzle.matches
    Sizzle.matchesSelector
    Sizzle.select
  */

  return Sizzle;

})(window);

jQuery.find = Sizzle;
```

Sizzle is added to the jQuery's source inside an IIFE, while its main function is returned and assigned to `jQuery.find` for use.

 For more information on Sizzle, you can visit
https://github.com/jquery/sizzle.

The Namespace Parameter Module variant

In this variant, instead of returning an object from our IIFE and then assigning it to the variable that acts as the Namespace of the Module, we create the Namespace and pass it as a parameter to the IIFE itself:

```
(function(simpleguid) {
  var guid;

  simpleguid.init = function() {
    guid = 1;
  };

  simpleguid.increaseCounter = function() {
    guid++;
  };

  simpleguid.getNext = function() {
    var nextGuid = guid;
    this.increaseCounter();
    return nextGuid;
  };

  simpleguid.init();
}) (window.simpleguid = window.simpleguid || {});
```

The last line of the Module definition tests whether the Module is already defined; in case it is not, it initializes it to an empty object literal and assigns it to the global object (`window`). In any case, the `simpleguid` parameter in the first line of the IIFE will hold the Module's Namespace.

The above expression is almost equivalent to writing:

```
window.simpleguid = window.simpleguid !== undefined ?
                    window.simpleguid : {};
```

Using the logical OR operator (||) makes the expression both shorter and more readable. Moreover, this is a pattern that most web developers have learned to easily recognize, and it appears in a lot of development patterns and best practices.

Once again, this pattern allows us to use the `this` keyword to access public members from within the exported methods of the Module. At the same time, it allows us to keep some functions and variables private, which will be accessible only by other functions of the Module.

Even though it's considered a good practice to define each Module to its own JS file, this variant also allows us to split the implementation of large Modules to more than one file. This benefit comes as a result of checking whether the Module is already defined, before initializing it to an empty object. This might be useful in some cases, with the only limitation being that each partial file of a Module can access the private members defined in its own IIFE.

Moreover, in order to avoid repetition, we can use a simpler identifier for the parameter of the IIFE and write our Module as follows:

```
(function(namespace) {
  /* … */

  namespace.getNext = function() {
    var nextGuid = guid;
    this.increaseCounter();
    return nextGuid;
  };

  namespace.init();
}) (window.simpleguid = window.simpleguid || {});
```

When it comes to applications with nested Namespaces, this pattern might start feeling a little uncomfortable to read. The last line of the Module definition will start to get longer for every extra level of nested namespacing that we define. For example, let's see how the `exports` submodule of our Todo application would look:

```
(function(exports) {
  var gDrivePublicKey = '#wnanqAASnsmkkw';

  exports.toGDrive = function() { /*...*/ };

  exports.toFile = function() { /*...*/ };

}) (myTodoApp.exports = myTodoApp.exports || {});
```

As you can see, each extra level of the nested Namespace needs to be added on both sides of the assignment that is passed as a parameter to the IIFE. For applications with complex features that lead to multiple levels of nested Namespaces, this could lead to Module definitions looking something like this:

```
(function(smallModule) {

    smallModule.method = function() { /*...*/ };

    return smallModule;
})(myApp.bigFeature.featurePart.smallModule =
    myApp.bigFeature.featurePart.smallModule || {});
```

Moreover, if we want to provide the same safety guaranties, as in the original code sample, then we would need to add similar safe checks for each Namespace level. With this in mind, the `exports` Module of our Todo application that we saw earlier would need to have the following form:

```
(function(exports) {
    var gDrivePublicKey = '#wnanqAASnsmkkw';

    exports.toGDrive = function() { /*...*/ };

    exports.toFile = function() { /*...*/ };

})((window.myTodoApp = window.myTodoApp || {},
    myTodoApp.exports = myTodoApp.exports || {}));
```

As seen in the preceding code, we used the comma operator (,) to separate each namespace existence check and wrapped the whole expression in an extra pair of parenthesis so that the whole expression is used as the first parameter of the IIFE. Using the comma operator (,) to join expressions will lead them to be evaluated in order and pass the result of the last evaluated expression as the parameter of the IIFE, and that result will be used as the Namespace of the Module. Keep in mind that, for each extra nested Namespace level, we need to add an extra existence check expression using the comma operator (,).

A disadvantage of this pattern, especially when used for nested namespacing, is that the Namespace definition of the Module is at the end of the file. Even though it is highly recommended to name your JS files so that they properly represent the Modules that they contain, for example, `mytodoapp.exports.js`; not having the Namespace near the top of the file can sometimes be counterproductive or misleading. An easy work-around for this problem would be to define the Namespace before the IIFE and then pass it as a parameter. For example, the preceding code using this technique would be transformed to something as follows:

```
window.myTodoApp = window.myTodoApp || {};
myTodoApp.exports = myTodoApp.exports || {};

(function(exports) {
  var gDrivePublicKey = '#wnanqAASnsmkkw';

  exports.toGDrive = function() { /*...*/ };

  exports.toFile = function() { /*...*/ };

})(myTodoApp.exports);
```

The IIFE-contained Module variant

Like in the previous variants of the Module Pattern, this variant does not actually have a specific variant name, but is recognized by the way the code is structured. The key concept of this variant is to move all the Module's code inside the IIFE:

```
(function() {

  window.simpleguid = window.simpleguid || {};

  var guid;

  simpleguid.init = function() {
    guid = 1;
  };

  simpleguid.increaseCounter = function() {
    guid++;
  };
```

```
simpleguid.getNext = function() {
  var nextGuid = guid;
  this.increaseCounter();
  return nextGuid;
};

simpleguid.init();
})();
```

This variant looks very similar to the previous one and mainly differs in the way that the Namespace is created. First of all, it keeps the Namespace check and initialization near the top of the Module, like a heading, making our code more readable regardless of whether we use a separate file for the Module or not. Like other variants of the Module Pattern, it supports private members for our Modules and also allows us to use the `this` keyword to access public methods and properties, making our code look more object-oriented.

Regarding implementations with nested Namespaces, the code structure of the `exports` submodule of our Todo application skeleton will look as follows:

```
(function() {
  window.myTodoApp = window.myTodoApp || {};
  myTodoApp.exports = myTodoApp.exports || {};

  var gDrivePublicKey = '#wnanqAASnsmkkw';

  myTodoApp.exports.toGDrive = function() { /*...*/ };

  myTodoApp.exports.toFile = function() { /*...*/ };

})();
```

As seen in the preceding code, we also borrowed the Namespace definition checks from the previous variant and, likewise, applied it to every level of nested namespacing. Even though this is not absolutely necessary, it brings the benefits that we discussed earlier such as enabling us to split a Module definition into several files and even results in a more error-tolerant implementation regarding the import order of the application's Modules.

The Revealing Module Pattern

The **Revealing Module Pattern** is a variant of the **Module Pattern** with a known and widely recognized name. What makes this pattern special is that it combines the best parts of the **Object Literal Pattern** and the **Module Pattern**. All the members of the Module are declared inside an IIFE, which at the end, returns an **Object Literal** containing only the public members of the Module and is assigned to the variable that acts as our Namespace:

```
var simpleguid = (function() {
  var guid = 1;

  function init() {
    guid = 1;
  }

  function increaseCounter() {
    guid++;
  }

  function getNext() {
    var nextGuid = guid;
    increaseCounter();
    return nextGuid;
  }

  return {
    init: init,
    getNext: getNext
  };
})();
```

One of the main benefits of this pattern that differentiates it from other variants is that it allows us to write all the code of our Module inside the IIFE, just like we would if they would be declared on the **Global Namespace**. Moreover, this pattern does not require any variation on the way that the public and private members are declared, making the code of the Module look uniform.

Since the returned Object Literal defines the publicly available members of the Module, it is also a convenient easy way to inspect its public API, even if it is written by someone else. Moreover, in case we need to expose a private method on our Module's API, all we need to do is add an extra property to the returned Object Literal without changing any part of its definition. Additionally, the use of an Object Literal enables us to change the exposed identifiers for the Module's API, without changing the names used by the Module's implementation internally.

Even if this is not clearly visible, the `this` keyword can be used for calls between the public members of the Module. Unfortunately, using the `this` keyword *is discouraged* for this pattern, since it breaks the uniformity of the function declarations and can easily lead to errors, especially when changing the visibility of a public method to private.

Since the Namespace definition is kept outside the body of the IIFE, this pattern clearly separates the Namespace definition from the actual implementation of the Module. Using this pattern to define a Module in a nested Namespace does not affect the Module's implementation, which will not look different at any point from a top-level Namespace Module. Rewriting the `exports` submodule of our Todo skeleton application using this pattern will make it look like this:

```
myTodoApp.exports = (function() {
  var gDrivePublicKey = '#wnanqAASnsmkkw';

  function toGDrive() { /*...*/ }

  function toFile() { /*...*/ }

  return {
    toGDrive: toGDrive,
    toFile: toFile
  };
})();
```

As a result of this separation, we have less code repetition and we can easily change the Namespace of a Module without affecting its implementation at all.

Using ES5 Strict Mode

A small but precious addition to all the Module Patterns that use IIFEs as their basic building blocks, is the use of **Strict Mode** for JavaScript execution. This was standardized in the fifth edition of JavaScript, and is an opt-in execution mode with slightly different semantics, in order to prevent some of the common pitfalls of JavaScript, but also having backwards compatibility in mind.

Under this mode, the JavaScript runtime engine will prevent you from accidentally creating a global variable and polluting the Global Namespace. Even in not-so-large applications, it is quite possible that a `var` declaration before the initial assignment of a variable can be missing, automatically promoting that to a global variable. To prevent this case, strict mode throws an error in case an assignment is issued to an undeclared variable. The following image show the error that is thrown by Firefox and Chrome when a Strict Mode violation happens.

```
» (function() {                                    > (function() {
      'use strict';                                      'use strict';
      x = 7; // this throws an error                     x = 7; // this throws an error
      // and the execution stops                         // and the execution stops
      console.log(x, window.x);                          console.log(x, window.x);
  })();                                              })();
× ReferenceError: assignment to undeclared variable x   ⊗ ▶ Uncaught ReferenceError: x is not defined(…)
```

This mode can be enabled by adding the `"use strict";` or `'use strict';` statement before any other statements. Even though this can be enabled on the global scope, it is highly recommended that you enable it only inside the scope of a function. Enabling it on the global scope might make third-party libraries that are non-strict-mode compliant stop working or misbehave. On the other hand, the best place to enable Strict Mode is inside the IIFE of a Module. The Strict Mode will be recursively applied to all nested Namespaces, methods, and functions of that IIFE.

> For more information on JavaScript's strict execution mode, you can visit `https://developer.mozilla.org/en-US/docs/Web/JavaScript/Reference/Strict_mode`.

Introducing ES6 Modules

Even though JavaScript initially had no built-in packaging and namespacing support like other programming languages, web developers filled the gaps by defining and adopting some design patterns for this purpose. These software development practices worked around the missing features of JavaScript and allowed large and scalable implementations of complex applications on a programming language that some years ago was mostly used for form validation.

This was until the 6th version of JavaScript, commonly referred to as ES6, was released as a standard on June 2015 and introduced the concept of Modules as part of the language.

ES6 is an abbreviation of ECMAScript 6th edition, which is also referred to as Harmony or ECMAScript 2015, where ECMAScript is the term that is used for the standardization process of JavaScript. The specification can be found at http://www.ecma-international.org/ecma-262/6.0/index.html#sec-modules.

As an example of ES6 Modules, we will see one of the many ways in which the `simpleguid` Module can be written:

```
var es6simpleguid = {};
export default es6simpleguid;

var guid;

es6simpleguid.init = function() {
  guid = 1;
};

es6simpleguid.increaseCounter = function() {
  guid++;
};

es6simpleguid.getNext = function() {
  var nextGuid = guid;
  this.increaseCounter();
  return nextGuid;
};

es6simpleguid.init();
```

If we save this as a file named `es6simpleguid.js`, then we can import and use it in a different file by simply writing the following code:

```
import es6simpleguid from 'es6simpleguid';
console.log(es6simpleguid.getNext());
```

Since **ES6 Modules** are by default in Strict Mode, writing your Modules today using your preferred Module Pattern variant with Strict Mode enabled will make your transition to ES6 Modules easier. Some of the above patterns require very few changes to achieve this. For example, in the IIFE-contained Module Pattern variant, all that is needed is remove the IIFE and the `"use strict"`; statement, replace the creation of the Module's Namespace with a variable, and use the `export` keyword on it.

Unfortunately, at the time of writing this book, no browser has 100% support for ES6 Modules. As a result, special loaders or tools that transpile ES6 to ES5 are required so that we can start writing our code using the new features of ES6.

 For more information, you can visit ES6 Module loader's documentation page at `https://github.com/ModuleLoader/es6-module-loader`, and Babel transpiler (earlier known as ES6toES5) at `http://babeljs.io/`.

Using Modules in jQuery applications

In order to demonstrate how the Module Pattern can lead to a better application structure, we will reimplement the dashboard example that we saw in the previous chapters. We will include all the functionalities that we have seen until now, including the counter of the open information boxes. The HTML and CSS code used is exactly the same as in the previous chapter and, as a result, our dashboard looks exactly the same as before:

For this demonstration, we will refactor our JavaScript code into four small Modules using the simple IIFE-contained Module variant. The `dashboard` Module will act as the main entry of code execution and also as the central coordination point of the dashboard application. The `categories` submodule will be responsible for the implementation of the upper-top part of our dashboard. This includes category selection, the presentation of appropriate buttons, and the handling of button clicks. The `informationBox` submodule will be responsible for the main part of our dashboard. It will provide methods to create and remove information boxes from the dashboard. Finally, the counter submodule will be responsible for keeping the field with the number of the currently open information boxes up-to-date, responding to the user actions.

A single change that we need to make to the HTML of the page in order to support this multimodule architecture is limited to the way in which the JavaScript files are included:

```html
<script type="text/javascript" src="jquery.js"></script>
<script type="text/javascript" src="dashboard.js"></script>
<script type="text/javascript" src="dashboard.categories.js"></script>
<script type="text/javascript" src="dashboard.informationbox.js">
</script>
<script type="text/javascript" src="dashboard.counter.js"></script>
```

 Even if this multifile structure makes the development and debugging processes a lot easier, it is recommended that we combine all these files before moving our application to a production environment. Several tools specialized for this job exist; for example, the very simple and effective grunt-contrib-concat project that is available at https://github.com/gruntjs/grunt-contrib-concat.

The main dashboard module

The resulting code for the dashboard module will look as follows:

```javascript
(function() {
    'use strict';

    window.dashboard = window.dashboard || {};

    dashboard.$container = null;

    dashboard.init = function() {
        dashboard.$container = $('.dashboardContainer');

        dashboard.categories.init();
        dashboard.informationBox.init();
        dashboard.counter.init();
    };

    $(document).ready(dashboard.init);
})();
```

As we already mentioned, the `dashboard` module will be the central point of our application. Since this is the starting point of execution for our application, its main duty is to do all the required initializations for itself and each submodule. The invocation of the `init()` method is wrapped inside a call to the `$(document).ready()` method so that its execution is delayed until the DOM tree of the page is fully loaded.

One important thing to note is that, during the initialization, we do a DOM traversal in order to find the container element of the dashboard and store it to a public property of the Module named `$container`. This element will be used by all the methods of the dashboard that need to access the DOM tree, in order to scope their code inside that container element, removing the need to constantly traverse the whole DOM tree using complex selectors. Keeping references to key DOM elements and reusing them in the different submodules, can make the application snappier and also lessen the chance of accidentally interfering with the rest of the page; thus, leading to less bugs that are also easier to resolve.

Cache elements but avoid memory leaks.

Keep in mind that maintaining references to DOM elements that are constantly added and removed from the page adds extra complexity to our application. This can even lead to memory leaks in case we are accidentally keeping a reference to an element that has already been removed from the page. For such elements, such as the information boxes, it might be safer and more effective to have delegated handling for the events triggered on them and to do a scoped DOM traversal when needed, in order to retrieve a jQuery object with fresh references of the elements.

The categories module

Let's proceed with the `categories` submodule:

```
(function() {
    'use strict';

    dashboard.categories = dashboard.categories || {};

    dashboard.categories.init = function() {
        dashboard.$container.find('#categoriesSelector')
            .change(function() {
                var $selector = $(this);
                var categoryIndex = +$selector.val();
```

```
                dashboard.categories.selectCategory(categoryIndex);
            });

        dashboard.$container.find('.dashboardCategories')
            .on('click', 'button', function() {
                var $button = $(this);
                var itemName = $button.text();
                dashboard.informationBox.openNew(itemName);
            });
    };

    dashboard.categories.selectCategory = function(categoryIndex) {
        var $dashboardCategories =
            dashboard.$container.find('.dashboardCategory');
        var $selectedItem =
            $dashboardCategories.eq(categoryIndex).show();
        $dashboardCategories.not($selectedItem).hide();
    };
})();
```

This submodule's initialization method uses the reference to the $container element that the main Module provides and adds two observers to the page. The first handles the change event on the <select> category and calls the selectCategory() method with the numeric value of the selected category. The selectCategory() method of this submodule will then handle revealing the appropriate category items, decoupling it from the event handling code and making it a reusable functionality available to the entire application.

Right after this, we create a single **Delegated Event Observer** that handles the click event on the <button> category item. It extracts the text of the <button> pressed and calls the openNew() method of the informationBox submodule that contains all the implementation related to information boxes. In a non-demo grade application, a parameter to such a method would probably be an identifier instead of a text value that would be used to retrieve more details from a remote server.

The informationBox module

The informationBox submodule that contains the implementation parts related to the main area of our dashboard has the following form:

```
(function() {
    'use strict';
```

```
dashboard.informationBox = dashboard.informationBox || {};

var $boxContainer = null;

dashboard.informationBox.init = function() {
    $boxContainer = dashboard.$container.find('.boxContainer');

    $boxContainer.on('click', '.boxCloseButton', function() {
        var $button = $(this);
        dashboard.informationBox.close($button);
    });
};

dashboard.informationBox.openNew = function(itemName) {
    var boxHtml = '<div class="boxsizer"><article class="box">' +
            '<header class="boxHeader">' +
                itemName +
                '<button class="boxCloseButton">&#10006;' +
                '</button>'+
            '</header>' +
            'Information box regarding ' + itemName +
        '</article></div>';
    $boxContainer.append(boxHtml);
};

dashboard.informationBox.close = function($boxElement) {
    $boxElement.closest('.boxsizer').remove();
};

})();
```

The first thing that this submodule's initialization code does is retrieve and store a reference of the container that holds the information boxes to the `$boxContainer` variable, using the `$container` property of the dashboard for scoping.

The `openNew()` method is responsible for creating the HTML required for a new information box and adding it to the dashboard using the `$boxContainer` variable, which acts like a private member of the Module, and is used for caching the reference of the previously assigned DOM element. This is a good practice that can improve the application's performance, since the stored element is never removed from the page and is used during the initialization and the `openNew()` methods of the Module. This way, we no longer need to execute slow DOM traversals every time the `openNew()` method is called.

The `close()` method, on the other hand, is responsible for removing an existing information box from the dashboard. It receives a jQuery composite collection object as a parameter related to the target information box, which is based on the way that the `$.fn.closest()` method works, and can either be the box element container or any of its descendants.

> Implementations of methods that provide flexibility regarding the way that they can be called can make them usable by more parts of a large application. The next logical step for this method, which is left as an exercise to the reader, would be to make it accept as a parameter, the index, or an identifier of the information box that needs to be closed.

The counter module

Lastly, here is how we rewrote the `counter` implementation, which we saw in the previous chapter, as an independent submodule:

```
(function() {
    'use strict';

    dashboard.counter = dashboard.counter || {};

    var dashboardItemCounter;
    var $counter;

    dashboard.counter.init = function() {
        $counter = $('#dashboardItemCounter');

        var $boxContainer = dashboard.$container
          .find('.boxContainer');
        var initialCount = $boxContainer.find('.boxsizer').length;
        dashboard.counter.setValue(initialCount);

        dashboard.$container.find('.dashboardCategories')
          .on('click', 'button', function() {
            dashboard.counter.setValue(dashboardItemCounter + 1);
        });

        $boxContainer.on('click', '.boxCloseButton', function() {
            dashboard.counter.setValue(dashboardItemCounter - 1);
        });
    };
```

```
dashboard.counter.setValue = function (value) {
    dashboardItemCounter = value;
    $counter.text(dashboardItemCounter);
};

})();
```

For this submodule, we are using the `$counter` variable as a private member to cache a reference to the element that displays the count. Another private member of the Module is the `dashboardItemCounter` variable, which at any point of time will hold the number of visible information boxes in the dashboard. Keeping such information on the members of our Modules reduces the times we need to reach the DOM tree to extract information on the state of the application, making the implementation more efficient.

 Preserving the state of the application in the properties of JavaScript objects or Modules instead of reaching the DOM to extract them, is a very good practice that makes the application's architecture more object-oriented, and is also adopted by most of the modern web development frameworks.

During the initialization of the Module, we are giving an initial value to our counter variable so that we are no longer dependent on the initial HTML of the page and have a more robust implementation. Moreover, we are attaching two **Delegated Event Observers**, one for clicks that will lead to the creation of new information boxes and another one for clicks that will close them.

Overview of the implementation

With the above, we completed the rewrite of the dashboard skeleton application to a modular architecture. All the available actions are exposed as public methods of each of our submodules that can be invoked programmatically and this way they are decoupled from the events that trigger them.

A good exercise for the reader would be to promote the decoupling even further, by also adopting the Publisher/Subscriber Pattern in the above implementation. The fact that the code is already structured into Modules will make such change a lot easier to implement.

Another part that can be implemented in a different way is the way in which the submodules are initialized. Instead of explicitly orchestrating the initialization of each Module in our main dashboard Module, we could instead initialize each submodule on its own by wrapping the invocation of the `init()` method in a `$(document).ready()` call and issuing its initialization right after its declaration. On the other hand, not having a central point to coordinate the initializations and relying on page events can feel less deterministic. Another way to implement it would be like the Publisher/Subscriber Pattern, by exposing a `registerForInit()` method on our main Module, which would keep track of the Modules that have been requested to be initialized using an array.

 For more jQuery code organization tips, you can visit `http://learn.jquery.com/code-organization/concepts/`.

Summary

In this chapter, we learned the concepts of Modules and Namespaces and also the benefits that come from their adoption in large applications. We had an in-depth analysis of the most widely adopted patterns and compared their benefits and limitations. We learned by example how to develop Modules using the Object Literal Pattern, the variants of the Module Pattern, and the Revealing Module Pattern.

We continued with a small introduction to ES5's Strict Mode and saw how it can benefit today's Modules. Then we proceeded by learning some details about the standardized but not yet widely supported **ES6 Modules**. Lastly, we saw how the architecture of the dashboard application can change dramatically after using the Module Pattern in its implementation.

Now that we have completed our introduction on how to use Modules and Namespaces, we can move on to the next chapter where we will be introduced to the facade pattern. In the next chapter, we will learn about the philosophy of facades and the uniform way that they define how code abstractions should be created so that they are easily understandable and reusable by other developers.

5
The Facade Pattern

In this chapter, we will showcase the **Facade Pattern**, a structural design pattern that tries to define a uniform way regarding how developers should create abstractions in their code. Initially, we will use this pattern to wrap complex APIs and expose simpler ones that focus on the needs of our application. We will see how jQuery embraces the concepts of this pattern in its implementation, how it achieves encapsulating complex implementations that are integral parts of the web developer's tool-belt into easy-to-use API's, and how this plays a critical role for its wide adoption.

In this chapter, we will:

- Introduce the Facade Pattern
- Document its key concepts and benefits
- See how jQuery uses it in its implementation
- Write an example implementation where Facades are used to completely abstract and decouple a third-party library

Introducing the Facade Pattern

The Facade is a structural software design pattern that deals with how abstractions of the various parts of an implementation should be created. The key concept of the Facade Pattern is to abstract an existing implementation and provide a simplified API that better matches the use cases of the developed application. According to most Computer Science bibliographies describing this pattern, a Facade is most commonly implemented as a specialized class that is used to segment the implementation of an application into smaller pieces of code, while providing an interface that completely hides the encapsulated complexity. In the web development world, it is also common to use plain objects or functions for the implementation of a Facade, taking advantage of the way in which JavaScript treats functions as objects.

In applications that have a modular structure, like the examples of the previous chapter, it is also common to implement Facades as separate modules with their own namespace. Moreover, for a larger implementation with very complex parts, an approach with multiple levels of Facades can also be followed. Once again, the Facades will be implemented as modules and submodules, having the top-level Facade orchestrating the methods of its submodules, while providing an API that completely hides the complexity of the entire subsystem.

The benefits of this pattern

Most of the time, the Facade Pattern is adopted for implementation parts that have a relatively high degree of complexity and are used in several places of an application, wherein large pieces of code can be replaced with a simple call to the created Facade, leading not only to less code repetition, but also helping us to increase the readability of the implementation. Since the Facade methods are usually named by the higher-level application concepts that they encapsulate, the resulting code is also easier to understand. The simplified API that a Facade provides through its convenient methods, leads to an implementation that is easier to use, understand, and also write unit tests for.

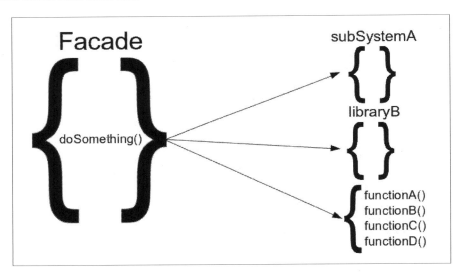

Moreover, having Facades to abstract complex implementations proves its usefulness in cases where there is a need to introduce a change to the business logic of the implementation. In case a Facade has a well-designed API with a prediction for future requirements, such changes can often require modifications just to the Facade's code, leaving the rest of the application's implementation untouched and following the **Separation of Concerns** principle.

In the same manner, using Facades to abstract the API of a third-party library to better match the needs of each application, provides a degree of decoupling between our code and the used library. In case the third-party library changes its API or needs to be replaced with another one, the different modules of the application will not need to be rewritten, since the implementation changes would be limited to the wrapper Facade. In this case, all that is needed is to provide an equivalent implementation using the new library API while keeping the Facade's API intact.

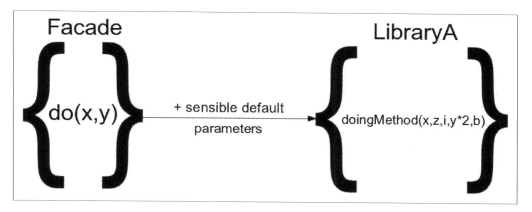

As an example of orchestrating method calls and using sensible defaults for specific use cases, take a look at the following sample implementation:

```
function do (x, y) {
  var z = y - x / 2;
  var yy = Math.pow(y, 2);
  var b = 3 * Math.random(); // add some randomness to the result
  var i = 0; // for this case
  return LibraryA.doingMethod(x, z, i, yy, b);
}
```

How it is adopted by jQuery

A very large part of the jQuery implementation is dedicated to providing simpler, shorter, and more convenient-to-use methods for things that the different JavaScript APIs already allow us to achieve, but with more lines of code and effort. By taking a look at the provided APIs of jQuery, we can distinguish some groups of related methods. This grouping can also be seen in the way in which the source code is structured, placing methods for related APIs near to each other.

Even if the word **Facade** does not appear in jQuery's source code, the use of this pattern can be witnessed by the way in which the related methods are defined on the exposed jQuery object. Most of the time, the related methods that form a group are implemented and defined as properties on an **Object Literal** and then attached to the jQuery object with a single call to the `$.extend()` or the `$.fn.extend()` method. As you might remember, from the beginning of this chapter, this matches almost exactly with the implementation that Computer Science commonly uses to describe how a Facade is implemented, with the exception that, in JavaScript, we can create a plain object without needing to first define a class. As a result, jQuery itself can be seen as a collection of Facades, where each one independently adds great value to the library with the API of convenient methods that it provides.

 For more information on `$.extend()` and `$.fn.extend()`, you can visit `http://api.jquery.com/jQuery.extend/` and `http://api.jquery.com/jQuery.fn.extend/`.

Some of the abstracted API groups that are big parts of the jQuery implementation and play a critical role to its adoption are as follows:

- The DOM Traversal API
- The AJAX API
- The DOM Manipulation API
- The Effects API

Also, a great example of how this pattern can be used to provide simplified APIs is jQuery's Events API, which provides a variety of convenient methods for the most common use cases that are easier to use than the respective plain JavaScript APIs.

The jQuery DOM Traversal API

At the time that jQuery was released, web developers could locate specific DOM elements of a page only by using the very limited `getElementById()` and `getElementsByTagName()` methods, since other methods, such as `getElementsByClassName()`, were not widely supported by the existing browsers. The jQuery team realized how the web development could be leveraged if there was a simple API that would ease such DOM traversals, which would work the same way across all browsers, be as effective as the familiar **CSS Selectors**, and did their best to make such an implementation a reality.

The result of this effort is the now famous jQuery DOM Traversal API that is exposed through the `$()` function, which played a serious role in the standardization of the `querySelectorAll()` method as part of the **Level 2 Selector API**. The implementation under the hood uses the methods provided by the **DOM API** and counts about 2,135 lines of code in jQuery v2.2.0, while it is even bigger in the v1.x versions that needed to support older browsers as well. As we saw in this chapter, because of its complexity this implementation is now part of a separate stand-alone project that is named **Sizzle**.

For more information on Sizzle and the `querySelectorAll()` method, you can visit `https://github.com/jquery/sizzle` and `https://developer.mozilla.org/en-US/docs/Web/API/document/querySelectorAll`.

Regardless of its complex implementation, the exposed APIs are quite easy to use, mostly using simple CSS Selectors as string parameters, making it an excellent example of how a Facade can be used to completely hide the complexity of its inner workings and expose a convenient API. Since Sizzle's API is still quite complex, the jQuery library actually wraps it with its own API acting as an extra Facade level:

```
// Line 733
function Sizzle( selector, context, results, seed ) { /* ... */ }

// Line 2678
jQuery.find = Sizzle;
```

The jQuery library first keeps a reference of Sizzle to the internal `jQuery.find()` method and then uses it to implement all its exposed DOM Traversal methods, which work on Composite Objects such as `$.fn.find()`:

```
// Line 2769
jQuery.fn.extend( {
  find: function( selector ) {
    /* 15 lines of code */
    for ( i = 0; i < len; i++ ) {
      jQuery.find( selector, self[ i ], ret );
    }
    /* 3 lines of code */
    return ret;
  }
} );
```

Finally, the famous $() function can actually be invoked in several ways, but even when it is invoked with a CSS Selector as a string parameter, it actually has an extra level of hidden complexity:

```
// Line 71
jQuery = function( selector, context ) {
  return new jQuery.fn.init( selector, context );
};

// Line 2825
rquickExpr = /^(?:\s*(<[\w\W]+>)[^>]*|#([\w-]*))$/,
// Line 2735
init = jQuery.fn.init = function( selector, context, root ) {
  /* 12 lines of code */
  if ( typeof selector === "string" ) {
    if (/* ... */) {
      /* 3 lines of code */
    } else {
      match = rquickExpr.exec( selector );
    }

    // Match html or make sure no context is specified for #id
    if ( match && ( match[ 1 ] || !context ) ) {
      if ( match[1] ) {
      /* 27 lines of code */
      // HANDLE: $(#id)
      } else {
        elem = document.getElementById( match[ 2 ] );

        // Support: Blackberry 4.6
        // gEBID returns nodes no longer in the document (#6963)
        if ( elem && elem.parentNode ) {
          // Inject the element directly into the jQuery object
          this.length = 1;
          this[ 0 ] = elem;
        }

        this.context = document;
        this.selector = selector;
        return this;
      }

    // HANDLE: $(expr, $(...))
    } else if ( !context || context.jquery ) {
```

```
        return ( context || root ).find( selector );

    // HANDLE: $(expr, context)
    // (which is just equivalent to: $(context).find(expr)
    } else {
        return this.constructor( context ).find( selector );
    }
} /* else ... 21 lines of code */
};
```

As you can see, in the preceding code, the `$()` is actually creating a new object with `$.fn.init()`. Instead of being just an entry point to `$.fn.find()` or `jQuery.find()`, it is actually a `Facade` that hides a level of optimization. Specifically, it makes jQuery faster by avoiding invoking `$.fn.find()` and Sizzle, when simple ID selectors are used by directly invoking the `getElementById()` method.

The property access and manipulation API

Another very interesting abstraction that follows the principles of the Facade Pattern and can be found in jQuery's source, is the `$.fn.prop()` method. Like the `$.fn.attr()`, `$.fn.val()`, `$.fn.text()`, and `$.fn.html()`, it belongs to a family of methods that is characterized by the fact that each method is both a getter and a setter of the related subject. The distinction of the method's execution mode is done by inspecting the number of parameters that are passed during its invocation. This convenient API allows us to have to remember less method signatures and make the setters differ only by one extra parameter. For example, `$('#myCheckBox').prop('checked')` will return true or false, based on the state of the selected checkbox. On the other hand, `$('#myCheckBox').prop('checked', true);` will programmatically check that checkbox for us. In the same concept, `$('button').prop('disabled', true);` will disable all the `<button>` elements on a page.

The `$.fn.prop()` method does the jQuery Composite Object handling, but the actual implementation of the Facade is the internal `jQuery.prop()` method. An extra concern that adds complexity to the Facade's implementation is the fact that there are some HTML attributes that have different identifiers for the corresponding properties on the DOM elements:

```
jQuery.extend( {

    prop: function( elem, name, value ) {
        /* 8 lies of code */
        if ( nType !== 1 || !jQuery.isXMLDoc( elem ) ) {
            // Fix name and attach hooks
            name = jQuery.propFix[ name ] || name;
```

```
        hooks = jQuery.propHooks[ name ];
    }

    if ( value !== undefined ) {
        if ( hooks && "set" in hooks &&
            ( ret = hooks.set( elem, value, name ) ) !== undefined ) {
            return ret;
        }
        return ( elem[ name ] = value );
    }

    if ( hooks && "get" in hooks &&
        ( ret = hooks.get( elem, name ) ) !== null ) {
        return ret;
    }
    return elem[ name ];
},

propHooks: {
    tabIndex: {
        get: function( elem ) {
            var tabindex = jQuery.find.attr( elem, "tabindex" );
            return tabindex ?parseInt( tabindex, 10 ) : /*...*/;
        }
    }
},

propFix: {
    "for": "htmlFor",
    "class": "className"
}
} );
```

The first highlighted code area efficiently resolves the property to attribute identifier mismatch by using the `propFix` and `propHooks` objects to do the matching. The `propFix` object acts like a simple dictionary to match the identifiers, while the `propHooks` object holds a function that does the matching in a less-hard-coded way, with programmatic testing. This is a generic implementation that can easily be extended by adding extra properties to those two objects.

The rest of the highlighted areas are responsible for the getter/setter mode of the method. The overall implementation is to perform the following tasks:

- Check whether a value is passed as an argument and, if the property finds that the assignment is successful, do the assignment and return the value.

- Alternatively, if there was no value passed, return the value of the requested property if it is retrievable.

Using Facades in our applications

In order to demonstrate how facades can be used both to encapsulate complexity, helping us enforce the Separation of Concerns principle, and also abstract third-party library APIs into more convenient methods that are application centric, we are going to demonstrate a very simple lottery application. Our "Element Lottery" application will populate its container with some Lottery Ticket elements that will have a unique ID and contain a random number.

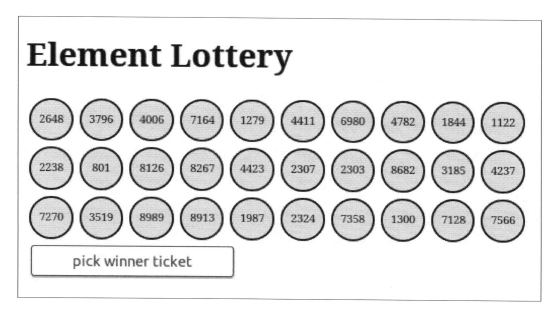

The winning ticket will be picked by randomly selecting one of the lottery elements, based on a random index among the created unique IDs. The winning number will then be announced to be the numeric content of the picked element. Let's see the modules of our application:

```
(function() {
  window.elementLottery = window.elementLottery || {};

  var elementIDs;
  var $lottery;
  var ticketCount = 30;

  elementLottery.init = function() {
    elementIDs = [];
    $lottery = $('#lottery').empty();
    elementLottery.add(ticketCount);
    $('#lotteryTicketButton').on('click', elementLottery.pick);
  };

  elementLottery.add = function(n) {
    for (var i = 0; i < n; i++) {
      var id = this.uidProvider.get();
      elementIDs.push(id);
      $lottery.append(this.ticket.createHtml(id));
    }
  };

  elementLottery.pick = function() {
    var index = Math.floor(Math.random() * elementIDs.length);
    var result = $lottery.find('#' + elementIDs[index]).text();
    alert(result);
    return result;
  };

  $(document).ready(elementLottery.init);
})();
```

The main `elementLottery` module of our application initialized itself right after the page was fully loaded. The `add` method is used to populate the lottery container element with tickets. It uses the `uidProvider` submodule to generate unique identifiers for the ticket elements, keeps track of them on the `elementIDs` array, uses the ticket submodule to construct the appropriate HTML code, and finally appends the element to the lottery. The `pick` method is used to randomly select the winning ticket by randomly selecting one of the generated identifiers, retrieving the page element with that ID, and displaying its content inside an alert box as the winning result. The `pick` method is triggered by clicking on the button that we have added an Observer during the initialization phase:

```
(function() {
  elementLottery.ticket = elementLottery.ticket || {};

  elementLottery.ticket.createHtml = function(id) {
    var ticketNumber = Math.floor(Math.random() * 1000 * 10);
    return '<div id="' + id + '" class="ticket">' + ticketNumber +
        '</div>';
  };
})();


(function() {
  elementLottery.uidProvider = elementLottery.uidProvider || {};

  elementLottery.uidProvider.get = function() {
    return 'Lot' + simpleguid.getNext();
  };
})();
```

The `ticket` submobule acts as a Facade with a single method that is used to
encapsulate the generation of a random number and the creation of the HTML
code that will be used as the ticket. On the other hand, the `uidProvide` submodule
is a Facade that provides a single get method that encapsulates the way we use the
`simpleguid` module that we saw in the previous chapters. As a result, we can easily
change the library that is used to generate unique identifiers and the only place
that we will have to modify the existing implementation will be the `uidProvide`
submodule. For example, let's see how it will look if we decided to use the
great node-uuid library that generates 128-bit unique identifiers as strings of
hexadecimal characters:

```
(function() {
  elementLottery.uidProvider = elementLottery.uidProvider || {};

  elementLottery.uidProvider.get = function() {
    return uuid.v4();
  };
})();
```

 For more information on the node-uui library, you can visit
https://github.com/broofa/node-uuid.

Summary

In this chapter, we learned what a Facade actually is. We learned its philosophy and the uniform way in which it defines how code abstractions should be created so that they are easily understandable and reusable by other developers.

Starting from the simplest use cases of this pattern, we learned how to wrap a complex API with a Facade and expose a simpler one that is focused on the needs of our application and is a better match to its specific use cases. We also saw how jQuery embraces the concepts of this pattern in its implementation and how providing simple APIs for more basic web-developing techniques, such as DOM Traversals, played a critical role for its wide adoption.

Now that we have completed our introduction to how the Facade Pattern can be used to decouple and abstract parts of an implementation, we can move on to the next chapter where we will be introduced to the Builder and Factory Patterns. In the next chapter, we will learn how to use these two Creational Design Patterns to abstract the process of generating and initializing new objects for specific use cases and analyze how their adoption can benefit our implementations.

6
The Builder and Factory Patterns

In this chapter, we will showcase the Builder and Factory Patterns, two of the most commonly used Creational Design Patterns. These two design patterns have some similarities with each other, share some common goals, and are dedicated to easing the creation of complex results. We will analyze the benefits that their adoption can bring to our implementations and also the ways in which they differ. Finally, we will learn how to use them properly and choose the most appropriate one for the different use cases of our implementations.

In this chapter, we will:

- Introduce the Factory Pattern
- See how the Factory Pattern is used by jQuery
- Have an example of the Factory Patten in a jQuery application
- Introduce the Builder Pattern
- Compare the Builder and Factory Patterns
- See how the Builder Pattern is used by jQuery
- Have an example of the Builder Patten in a jQuery application

Introducing the Factory Pattern

The Factory Pattern is part of the group of Creational Patterns and overall it describes a generic way for object creation and initialization. It is commonly implemented as an object or function that is used to generate other objects. According to the majority of Computer Science resources, the reference implementation of the Factory Pattern is described as a class that provides a method that returns newly created objects. The returned objects are commonly the instances of a specific class or subclass, or they expose a set of specific characteristics.

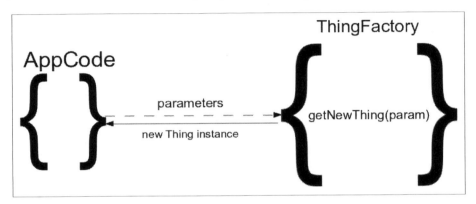

The key concept of the Factory pattern is to abstract the way an object or a group of related objects are created and initialized for a specific purpose. The point of this abstraction is to avoid coupling an implementation with specific classes or the way that each object instance needs to be created and configured. The result is an implementation that works as an abstract way for object creation and initialization, which follows the concept of Separation of Concerns.

The resulting implementations are only based on the object methods and properties that are required by their algorithm or business logic. Such an approach can benefit the modularity and extensibility of an implementation, by following the concept of programming over Object Features and Functionality instead of Object Classes. This gives us the flexibility to change the used classes with any other object that exposes the same functionality.

How it is adopted by jQuery

As we have already noted in the earlier chapters, one of the early goals of jQuery was to provide a solution that worked the same across all browsers. The 1.12.x version series of jQuery are focused on providing support for browsers as old as Internet Explorer 6 (IE6), while maintaining the same API with the newer v2.2.x versions that only focus on modern browsers.

In order to have a similar structure and maximize the common code between the two versions, the jQuery team tried to abstract most compatibility mechanisms in a different implementation layer. Such a development practice greatly improves the readability of the code and reduces the complexity of the main implementation, encapsulating it into different smaller pieces.

A great example of this is the implementation of the AJAX-related methods that jQuery provides. Specifically, in the following code, you can find a part of it, as found in version 1.12.0 of jQuery:

```
// Create the request object
// (This is still attached to ajaxSettings for backward compatibility)
jQuery.ajaxSettings.xhr = window.ActiveXObject !== undefined ?
  // Support: IE6-IE8
  function() {

    // XHR cannot access local files, always use ActiveX for that case
    if ( this.isLocal ) {
      return createActiveXHR();
    }
    // Support: IE 9-11
    if ( document.documentMode > 8 ) {
      return createStandardXHR();
    }
    // Support: IE<9
    return /^(get|post|head|put|delete|options)$/i.test( this.type )
      && createStandardXHR() || createActiveXHR();

  } :
  // For all other browsers, use the standard XMLHttpRequest object
  createStandardXHR;

// Functions to create xhrs
function createStandardXHR() {
  try {
    return new window.XMLHttpRequest();
  } catch ( e ) {}
}

function createActiveXHR() {
  try {
    return new window.ActiveXObject( "Microsoft.XMLHTTP" );
  } catch ( e ) {}
}
```

Every time a new AJAX request is issued on jQuery, the `jQuery.ajaxSettings.xhr` method is used as a Factory that creates a new instance of the appropriate XHR object based on the support of the current browser. Looking in more detail, we can see that the `jQuery.ajaxSettings.xhr` method orchestrates the use of two smaller Factory functions, with each responsible for a specific implementation of AJAX. Moreover, we can see that it actually tries to avoid running the compatibility tests on every call by directly wiring up its reference to the smaller `createStandardXHR` Factory function when appropriate.

Using Factories in our applications

As an example use case of Factories, we will create a data-driven form where our users will be able to fill some fields that are dynamically created and inserted into the page. We will assume the existence of an array containing objects that describe each form field that needs to be presented. Our Factory method will encapsulate the way in which each form field needs to be constructed, and properly handle each specific case, based on the characteristics defined on the related objects.

Data Driven Form

Firt Name:

Last Name:

e-mail address:

Date of birth:

Years of experience:

Summary:

Receive notification e-mails: ☐

By using this form you accept the terms of use

save!

submit!

The HTML code for this page is quite simple:

```
<h1>Data Driven Form</h1>

<form></form>

<script type="text/javascript" src="jquery.js"></script>
<script type="text/javascript"
  src="datadrivenform.js"></script>
```

It only contains an `<h1>` element with the page heading and an empty `<form>` element that will host the generated fields. As for the CSS used, we only style the `<button>` elements in the same way as we did in the previous chapters.

As for the JavaScript implementation of the application, we create a module and declare `dataDrivenForm` as the namespace of this example. This module will contain the data that describes our form, the Factory method that will generate the HTML of each form element and, of course, the initialization code that will combine the aforementioned parts to create the resulting form:

```
(function() {
  'use strict';

  window.dataDrivenForm = window.dataDrivenForm || {};

  dataDrivenForm.formElementHTMLFactory =
   function (type, name, title) {
    if (!title || !title.length) {
      title = name;
    }
    var topPart = '<div><label><span>' + title + ':</span><br />';
    var bottomPart = '</label></div>';
    if (type === 'text') {
      return topPart +
        '<input type="text" maxlength="200" name="' +
          name + '" />' +
        bottomPart;
    } else if (type === 'email') {
      return topPart +
        '<input type="email" required name="' + name + '" />' +
        bottomPart;
    } else if (type === 'number') {
      return topPart +
        '<input type="number" min="0" max="2147483647" ' +
          'name="' + name + '" />' +
```

```
          bottomPart;
      } else if (type === 'date') {
        return topPart +
          '<input type="date" min="1900-01-01" name="' +
            name + '" />' +
          bottomPart;
      } else if (type === 'textarea') {
        return topPart +
          '<textarea cols="30" rows="3" maxlength="800" name="' +
            name + '" />' +
          bottomPart;
      } else if (type === 'checkbox') {
        return '<div><label><span>' + title + ':</span>' +
          '<input type="checkbox" name="' + name + '" />' +
          '</label></div>';
      } else if (type === 'notice') {
        return '<p>' + name + '</p>';
      }  else if (type === 'button') {
        return '<button name="' + name + '">' + title + '!</button>';
      }
    };

})();
```

Our Factory method will be invoked with three parameters. Starting from the most important one, it accepts the `type` and the `name` of the form field and also the `title` that will be used as its description. Since most form fields share some common characteristics, like their title, the Factory method tries to abstract them in order to have less code repetition. As you can see, the Factory method also contains some sensible extra configuration for each field type, like the `maxlength` attribute of the text fields, that is specific for this use case.

The object structure that will be used to represent each form element will be a plain JavaScript object that has a `type`, `name`, and `title` property. The collection of objects that describe the form fields will be grouped in an array and be available on the `dataDrivenForm.parts` property of our module. In a real-world application, these fields would commonly either be retrieved with an AJAX request or be injected into some part of the HTML of the page. In the following code snippet, we can see the data that will be used to drive the creation of our form:

```
dataDrivenForm.parts = [{
    type: 'text',
    name: 'firstname',
    title: 'First Name'
}, {
```

```
    type: 'text',
    name: 'lastname',
    title: 'Last Name'
}, {
    type: 'email',
    name: 'email',
    title: 'e-mail address'
}, {
    type: 'date',
    name: 'birthdate',
    title: 'Date of birth'
}, {
    type: 'number',
    name: 'experience',
    title: 'Years of experience'
}, {
    type: 'textarea',
    name: 'summary',
    title: 'Summary'
}, {
    type: 'checkbox',
    name: 'receivenotifications',
    title: 'Receive notification e-mails'
}, {
    type: 'notice',
    name: 'By using this form you accept the terms of use'
}, {
    type: 'button',
    name: 'save'
}, {
    type: 'button',
    name: 'submit'
}];
```

Finally, we define and immediately invoke an `init` method for our module:

```
dataDrivenForm.init = function() {
  for (var i = 0; i < dataDrivenForm.parts.length; i++) {
    var part = dataDrivenForm.parts[i];
    var elementHTML = dataDrivenForm.formElementHTMLFactory(
      part.type, part.name, part.title);
    // check if the result is null, undefined or empty string
    if (elementHTML && elementHTML.length) {
      $('form').append(elementHTML);
    }
```

```
    }
};
```

```
$(document).ready(dataDrivenForm.init);
```

The initialization code waits until the DOM of the page is fully loaded and then uses the Factory method to create the form elements and attach them to the `<form>` element of our page. An extra concern of the preceding code is to check the result of the Factory method invocation before actually starting to use it.

Most Factories, when invoked with parameters for a case they can't handle, return `null` or empty objects. As a result, it's a good common practice, when using Factories, to check whether the result of each invocation is actually valid.

As you can see, having Factories that accept only simple parameters (for example, strings and numbers), in many cases, leads to an increased number of parameters. Even though these parameters may only be used in specific cases, the API of our Factory starts to be awkwardly long and needs proper documentation for each special case in order to be usable.

Ideally, a Factory method should accept as few arguments as possible, otherwise it will start looking like a Facade that only provides a different API. Since, in some cases, using a single string or numeric argument does not suffice, in order to avoid using a huge number of parameters, we can follow a practice where the Factory is designed to accept a single object as its parameter.

For example, in our case, we can just pass the whole object that describes the form field as a parameter to the Factory method:

```
dataDrivenForm.formElementHTMLFactory = function
(formElementDefinition) {
  var topPart = '<div><label><span>' +
    formElementDefinition.title + ':</span><br />';
  var bottomPart = '</label></div>';
  if (formElementDefinition.type === 'text') {
    return topPart +
      '<input type="text" maxlength="200" name="' +
        formElementDefinition.name + '" />' +
      bottomPart;
  } /* ... */
};
```

This practice is suggested for the following cases:

* When we create generic Factories that are not focused on specific use cases and we need to configure their results differently for each specific use case.

- When the constructed objects have many optional configuration parameters that largely differ. In this case, adding them as separate parameters to the Factory method would lead to invocations that have a number of `null` arguments, depending on which exact argument we are interested in defining.

Another practice, especially in JavaScript programming, is to create a Factory method that accepts a simple string or numeric value as its first argument and optionally provide a complementary object as a second parameter. This enables us to have a simple generic API that can be use-case-specific and also gives us some extra points of freedom to configure some special cases. This approach is used by the `$.ajax( url [, settings ] )` method that allows us to generate simple GET requests by just providing a URL and also accepts an optional `settings` parameter that allows us to configure any aspect of the request. Changing the above implementation to use this variation is left as an exercise for the reader, in order to experiment and get familiar with the use of Factory methods.

Introducing the Builder Pattern

The Builder Pattern is part of the group of Creational Patterns and provides us a way to create objects that require a lot of configuration before they reach the point where they can be used. The Builder Pattern is often used for objects that accept many optional parameters in order to define their operation. Another matching case is for the creation of objects where their configuration needs to be done in several steps or in a specific order.

The common paradigm for the Builder Pattern according to Computer Science is that there is a Builder Object that provides one or more setter methods (`setA(...)`, `setB(...)`) and a single generation method that constructs and returns the newly created result object (`getResult()`).

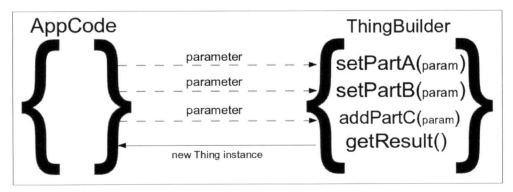

This pattern has two important concepts. The first one is that the Builder Object exposes a number of methods as a way to configure the different parts of the object that is under construction. During the configuration phase, the Builder Object preserves an internal state that reflects the effects of the invocations of the provided setter methods. This can be beneficial when used to create objects that accept a large number of configuration parameters, solving the problem of Telescopic Constructors.

> Telescopic Constructors is an anti-pattern of object-oriented programming that describes the situation where a class provides several constructors that tend to differ on the number, the type, and the combination of the arguments that they require. Object classes with several parameters that can be used in many different combinations can often lead to implementations falling into this anti-pattern.

The second important concept is that it also provides a generation method that returns the actual constructed object based on the preceding configuration. Most of the time, the instantiation of the requested object is done lazily and actually takes place at the moment that this method is invoked. In some cases, the Builder Object allows us to invoke the generation method more than once, allowing us to generate several objects with the same configuration.

How it is adopted by jQuery's API

The Builder Pattern can also be found as part of the API that jQuery exposes. Specifically, the jQuery $() function can also be used to create new DOM elements by invoking it with an HTML string as an argument. As a result, we can create new DOM elements and set their different parts as we need them, instead of having to create the exact HTML string that is needed for the final result:

```
var $input = $('<input />');
$input.attr('type','number');
$input.attr('min', '0');
$input.attr('max', '100');
$input.prop('required', true);
$input.val(4);

$input.appendTo('form');
```

The `$('<input />')` call returns a Composite Object containing an element that is not attached to the DOM tree of the page. This unattached element is only an in-memory object that is neither fully constructed nor fully functional until we attach it to the page. In this case, this Composite Object acts like a Builder Object Instance having an internal state of objects that are not yet finalized. Right after this, we do a series of manipulations on it using some jQuery methods that act like the setter methods described by the Builder Pattern.

Finally, after we apply all the required configurations, so that the resulting object behaves in the desired way, we invoke the `$.fn.appendTo()` method. The `$.fn.appendTo()` method works as the generation method of the Builder Pattern, by attaching the in-memory element of the `$input` variable to the DOM tree of the page, transforming it into an actual attached DOM element.

Of course, the above example can get more readable and less repetitive by utilizing the Fluent API that jQuery provides for its methods, and also combine the `$.fn.attr()` method invocations. Moreover, jQuery allows us to use almost all its methods to do traversals and manipulations on the elements that are under construction, just as we can on normal DOM element Composite Objects. As a result, the above example can get a little more complete as follows:

```
$('<input />').attr({
    'type':'number',
    'min': '0',
    'max': '100'
})
.prop('required', true)
.val(4)
.css('display', 'block')
.wrap('<label>') // wrap the input with a <label>
.parent() // traverse one level up, to the <label>
.prepend('<span>Qty:#</span>')
.appendTo('form');
```

The result will look as follows:

The criteria that allow us to categorize this overloaded way of invoking the $() function as an implementation that adopts the Builder Pattern, is the fact that:

- It returns an object with an internal state containing partially constructed elements. The contained elements are only in-memory objects that are not part of the page's DOM tree.

- It provides us methods to manipulate its internal state. Most jQuery methods can be used for this purpose.

- It provides us method(s) to generate the final result. We can use jQuery methods such as $.fn.appendTo() and $.fn.insertAfter(), as a way to complete the construction of the internal elements and make them part of the DOM tree with properties that reflect their earlier in-memory representation.

As we have already seen in *Chapter 1, A Refresher on jQuery and the Composite Pattern*, the primary way to use the $() function is to invoke it with a CSS selector as a string parameter and in turn it will retrieve the matching page elements and return them in a Composite Object. On the other hand, when the $() function detects that it has been invoked with a string parameter that looks like a piece of HTML, it works as a DOM element Builder. This overloaded way of invoking the $() function bases its detection on the assumption that the provided HTML code starts and ends with the inequality symbols < and >:

```
init = jQuery.fn.init = function( selector, context ) {
  /* 11 lines of code */
  // Handle HTML strings
  if ( typeof selector === "string" ) {
    if ( selector[ 0 ] === "<" &&
        selector[ selector.length - 1 ] === ">" &&
        selector.length >= 3 ) {
      // Assume that strings that start and end with <> are HTML
      // and skip the regex check
      match = [ null, selector, null ];

    } /*...*/


    // Match html or make sure no context is specified for #id
    if ( match && ( match[ 1 ] || !context) ) {
```

```
        // HANDLE: $(html) -> $(array)
      if ( match[ 1 ] ) {
        /* 4 lines of code */
        jQuery.merge( this,
          jQuery.parseHTML( match[ 1 ], /*...*/ ) );
        /* 16 lines of code */

        return this;
      }/*...*/
    }/*...*/
  }/*...*/
};
```

As we can see in the preceding code, this overload uses the `jQuery.parseHTML()` helper method that ultimately leads to a call of the `createDocumentFragment()` method. The created **Document Fragment** is then used as a host of the under construction tree structure of elements. After jQuery finishes converting the HTML into elements, the Document Fragment is discarded and only it's hosted elements are returned:

```
jQuery.parseHTML = function( data, context, keepScripts ) {
  /* 17 lines of code */
  // Single tag
  if ( parsed ) {
    return [ context.createElement( parsed[ 1 ] ) ];
  }

  parsed = buildFragment( [ data ], context, scripts );
  /* 5 lines of code */
  return jQuery.merge( [], parsed.childNodes );
};
```

This results in the creation of a new jQuery Composite Object containing an in-memory tree structure of elements. Even though these elements are not attached to the actual DOM tree of the page, we can still do traversals and manipulations on them like any other jQuery Composite Object.

 For more information on Document Fragments, you can visit: https://developer.mozilla.org/en-US/docs/Web/API/ Document/createDocumentFragment.

How it is used by jQuery internally

An undoubtedly big part of jQuery is its AJAX-related implementation, which aims to provide a simple API for asynchronous calls that is also configurable to a large degree. Using the jQuery Source Viewer and searching for `jQuery.ajax`, or directly searching jQuery's source code for `"ajax:"`, will bring us the aforementioned implementation. In order to make its implementation more straightforward and also allow it to be configurable, jQuery internally uses a special object structure that acts as a Builder Object for the creation and handling of each AJAX request. As we will see, this is not the most common way of using a Builder Object, but it is actually a special variant with some modifications in order to fit the requirements of this complex implementation:

```
jqXHR = {
  readyState: 0,

  // Builds headers hashtable if needed
  getResponseHeader: function( key ) {/* ... */},

  // Raw string
  getAllResponseHeaders: function() {/* ... */},

  // Caches the header
  setRequestHeader: function( name, value ) {/* ... */},

  // Overrides response content-type header
  overrideMimeType: function( type ) {/* ... */},

  // Status-dependent callbacks
  statusCode: function( map ) {/* ... */},

  // Cancel the request
  abort: function( statusText ) {/* ... */}
};
```

The main method that the `jqXHR` object exposes to configure the generated asynchronous request is the `setRequestHeader()` method. The implementation of this method is quite generic, enabling jQuery to set all the different HTTP headers for the request, using only one method.

In order to provide an even greater degree of flexibility and abstraction, jQuery internally uses a separate `transport` object as a wrapper of the `jqXHR` object. This transport object handles the part of actually sending the AJAX request to the server, working like a *partner builder object* that cooperates with the `jqXHR` object for the creation of the final result. This way, jQuery can fetch Scripts, XML, JSON, and JSONP responses from the same or cross-origin servers, using the same API and overall implementation:

```
transport = inspectPrefiltersOrTransports( transports, s, options,
    jqXHR );

// If no transport, we auto-abort
if ( !transport ) {
  done( -1, "No Transport" );
} else {
  jqXHR.readyState = 1;
  /* 12 lines of code */
  try {
    state = 1;
    transport.send( requestHeaders, done );
  } catch ( e ) {/* 7 lines of code */}
}
```

Another special thing about this implementation of the Builder Pattern is that it should be able to operate in both synchronous and asynchronous manner. As a result, the `send()` method of the `transport` object that acts as the result generator method of the wrapped `jqXHR` object can't just return a result object, but it is instead invoked with a callback.

Finally, after the request is complete, jQuery uses the `getResponseHeader()` method to retrieve all the required response headers. Right after this, the headers are used to properly convert the received response that is stored in the `responseText` property of the `jqXHR` object.

How to use it in our applications

As an example use case of the Builder Pattern in a client-side application that uses jQuery, we will create a simple data-driven multiple-choice quiz. The main reason that the Builder Pattern is a better match for this case, as compared to the Factory Pattern example that we saw earlier, is that the result is more complex and has more degrees of configuration. Each question will be generated based on a model object that will represent its desired properties.

Data Driven Quiz

Which is the most preferred way to write our JavaScript code?

- ○ inline along with our HTML
- ○ flat inside *.js files
- ○ in small Modules, one per *.js file

What does the $() function returns when invoked with a CSS selector?

- ○ a single element
- ○ an array of elements
- ○ the HTML of the selected element
- ○ a Composite Object

Which of the following are Design Patterns

- ☐ Garbage Collector
- ☐ Class
- ☐ Object Literal
- ☐ Observer

How can get a hold to the <body> element of a page?

- ☐ document.body
- ☐ document.getElementsByTagName('body')[0]
- ☐ $('body')[0]
- ☐ document.querySelector('body')

Once again, the required HTML is very simple, containing just an `<h1>` element with the header of the page, an empty `<form>` tag, and some references to our CSS and JavaScript resources:

```
<h1>Data Driven Quiz</h1>
<form> </form>

<script type="text/javascript" src="jquery.js"></script>
<script type="text/javascript" src="datadrivenquiz.js"></script>
```

Besides the common, simple styles that we have seen in the previous chapters, the CSS of this example additionally defines:

```
ul.unstyled > li {
    margin: 0;
    padding: 0;
    list-style: none;
}
```

For the needs of this example, we will create a module with a new namespace named dataDrivenQuiz. As we saw earlier in this chapter, we will assume the existence of an array containing the model objects that describe each multiple-choice question that needs to be presented. Each of these model objects will have:

- A title property that will hold the question

- An options property that will be an array with the available answers to choose from

- An optional acceptsMultiple property to signify whether we should use radio or check boxes

The array with the model objects that describe the form questions will be available at the dataDrivenQuiz.parts property of our module, while keeping in mind that our implementation could easily be modified to fetch the models with an AJAX request:

```
dataDrivenQuiz.questions = [{
  title: 'Which is the most preferred way to write our JavaScript
code?',
  options: [
    'inline along with our HTML',
    'flat inside *.js files',
    'in small Modules, one per *.js file'
  ]
}, {
  title: 'What does the $() function returns when invoked with a CSS
selector?',
  options: [
    'a single element',
    'an array of elements',
    'the HTML of the selected element',
    'a Composite Object'
  ]
}, {
  title: 'Which of the following are Design Patterns',
  acceptsMultiple: true,
  options: [
```

```
        'Garbage Collector',
        'Class',
        'Object Literal',
        'Observer'
    ]
}, {
    title: 'How can get a hold to the <body> element of a page?',
    acceptsMultiple: true,
    options: [
        'document.body',
        'document.getElementsByTagName(\'body\')[0]',
        '$(\'body\')[0]',
        'document.querySelector(\'body\')'
    ]
}];
```

 Defining the data structures that are required to describe a problem, before starting the actual implementation, allows us to focus on the needs of the application and get an estimate of its overall complexity.

Given the preceding sample data, let's now proceed to the implementation of our Builder:

```
function MultipleChoiceBuilder() {
    this.title = 'Untitled';
    this.options = [];
}
dataDrivenQuiz.MultipleChoiceBuilder = MultipleChoiceBuilder;

MultipleChoiceBuilder.prototype.setTitle = function(title) {
    this.title = title;
    return this;
};

MultipleChoiceBuilder.prototype.setAcceptsMultiple =
    function(acceptsMultiple) {
        this.acceptsMultiple = acceptsMultiple;
        return this;
    };

MultipleChoiceBuilder.prototype.addOption = function(title) {
    this.options.push(title);
    return this;
```

```
  };

  MultipleChoiceBuilder.prototype.getResult = function() {
    var $header = $('<header>').text(this.title || 'Untitled');

    var questionGuid = 'quizQuestion' + (jQuery.guid++);
    var $optionsList = $('<ul class="unstyled">');
    for (var i = 0; i < this.options.length; i++) {
      var $input = $('<input />').attr({
        'type': this.acceptsMultiple ? 'checkbox' : 'radio',
        'value': i,
        'name': questionGuid,
      });

      var $option = $('<li>');
      $('<label>').append($input, $('<span>').text(this.options[i]))
        .appendTo($option);
      $optionsList.append($option);
    }
    return $('<article>').append($header, $optionsList);
  };
```

Using the Prototypical Object-Oriented approach of JavaScript, we firstly define the Constructor Function for our MultipleChoiceBuilder class. When the Constructor Function is invoked using the new operator, it will create a new instance of the Builder and initialize its title property to "Untitled" and the options property to an empty array.

Right after this, we complete the definition of the Constructor Function of our Builder, we attach it as a member of our module, and continue with the definition of its setter methods. Following the Prototypical Class paradigm, the setTitle(), setAcceptsMultiple(), and addOption() methods are defined as properties of our Builder's Prototype and are used to modify the internal state of the under construction element. Additionally, in order to enable us to chain several invocations of these methods, which results in a more readable implementation, all of them end with the return this; statement.

We complete the implementation of the Builder with the getResult() method that has the duty of gathering all the parameters that are applied on the Builder object instance and generating the resulting element wrapped inside a jQuery Composite Object. In its first line, it creates a header of the question. Right after this, it creates a <ul> element with the unstyled CSS class to hold the possible answers to the question and a unique identifier that will be used as the name of the generated <input> of the question.

In the for loop that follows, we will:

- Create an `<input />` element for each option of the question
- Properly set its `type` as a `checkbox` or a `radio` button, based on the value of the `acceptsMultiple` property
- Use the for loop's iteration number as its `value`
- Set the unique identifier that we generated earlier for the question as the input's `name` in order to group the answers
- Finally, add a `<label>` with the option's text, which wraps all of them inside an `<li>`, and append it to the question's `<ul>`.

Lastly, the header and the list of options are wrapped in an `<article>` element, which is then returned as the final result of the Builder.

In the above implementation, we use the `$.fn.text()` method to assign the content of the question's header and its available choices instead of string concatenation, in order to properly escape the `<` and `>` characters that are found in their descriptions. As an extra note, since some of the answers also contain single quotes, we need to escape them in the model objects using a backslash (`\ '`).

Finally, in our module's implementation, we define and immediately invoke the `init` method:

```
dataDrivenQuiz.init = function() {
  for (var i = 0; i < dataDrivenQuiz.questions.length; i++) {
    var question = dataDrivenQuiz.questions[i];
    var builder = new dataDrivenQuiz.MultipleChoiceBuilder();

    builder.setTitle(question.title)
      .setAcceptsMultiple(question.acceptsMultiple);

    for (var j = 0; j < question.options.length; j++) {
      builder.addOption(question.options[j]);
    }

    $('form').append(builder.getResult());
  }
};

$(document).ready(dataDrivenQuiz.init);
```

The execution of the initialization code is delayed until the DOM tree of the page is fully loaded. Then the `init()` method iterates over the model objects array and uses the Builder to create each question and populate the `<form>` element of our page.

A good exercise for the reader would be to extend the above implementation in order to support the client-side evaluation of the quiz. Firstly, this would require you to extend the question objects to contain information about the validity of each choice. Then, it would be suggested that you create a Builder that would retrieve the answers from the form, evaluate them, and create a result object with the user choices and the overall success on the quiz.

Summary

In this chapter, we learned the concepts of the Builder and Factory Patterns, two of the most commonly used Creational Design Patterns. We analyzed their common goals, their different approaches on abstracting the process of generating and initializing new objects for specific use cases, and how their adoption can benefit our implementations. Finally, we learned how to use them properly and how to choose the most appropriate one for the different use cases of any given implementations.

Now that we have completed our introduction to the most important Creational Design Patterns, we can move on to the next chapter where we will be introduced to the development patterns that are used to program asynchronous and concurrent procedures. In more detail, we will learn how to orchestrate the execution of asynchronous procedures that run either in order or parallel to each other, by using callbacks and jQuery Deferred and Promises APIs.

7
Asynchronous Control Flow Patterns

This chapter is dedicated to development patterns that are used to ease the programming of asynchronous and concurrent procedures.

At first, we will have a refresher on how Callbacks are used in JavaScript programming and how they are an integral part of web development. We will then proceed and identify their benefits and limitations when used in large and complex implementations.

Right after this, we will be introduced to the concept of Promises. We will learn how jQuery's Deferred and Promise APIs work and how they differ from ES6 Promises. We will see where and how they are used internally by jQuery to simplify its implementation and lead to more readable code. We will analyze their benefits, classify the best matching use cases, and compare them with the classic Callback Pattern.

By the end of this chapter, we will be able to use jQuery Deferred and Promises to efficiently orchestrate the execution of asynchronous procedures that run either in order or parallel to each other.

In this chapter, we will:

- Have a refresher on how Callbacks are used in JavaScript programming
- Get introduced to the concept of Promises
- Learn how to use jQuery's Deferred and Promise APIs
- Compare jQuery Promises with ES6 Promises
- Learn how to orchestrate asynchronous tasks using Promises.

Programming with callbacks

A Callback can be defined as a function that is passed as an invocation argument to another function or method (which is referred to as a Higher-Order Function) and is expected to be executed at some later point of time. In this way, the piece of code that was handed our Callback will eventually invoke it, propagating the results of an operation or event back to the context that the Callback was defined.

Callbacks can be characterized as synchronous or asynchronous, based on the way that the invoked method operates. A Callback is characterized as synchronous when it is executed by a blocking method. On the other hand, JavaScript developers are more familiar with **asynchronous callbacks**, also called **deferred callbacks**, which are set to be executed after an asynchronous procedure finishes or when a specific event occurs (page load, click, AJAX response arrival, and so on).

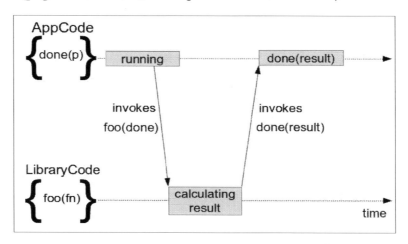

Callbacks are widely used in JavaScript applications since they are an integral part of many core JavaScript APIs such as AJAX. Moreover, JavaScript implementations of this pattern are almost word for word as described by the above simple definition. This is a result of the way that JavaScript treats functions as objects and allows us to store and pass method references as simple variables.

Using simple callbacks in JavaScript

Perhaps one of the simplest examples of asynchronous callbacks in JavaScript is the `setTimeout()` function. The following code demonstrates a simple use of it, where we invoke `setTimeout()` with the `doLater()` function as a callback parameter and, after 1000 milliseconds of waiting, the `doLater()` callback is invoked:

```
var alertMessage = 'One second passed!';
function doLater() {
    alert(alertMessage);
}
setTimeout(doLater, 1000);
```

As seen in the simple preceding example, the callback is executed in the context that it was defined. The callback still has access to the variables of the context that it was defined by creating a closure. Even though the preceding example uses a named function defined earlier, the same applies for anonymous callbacks:

```
var alertMessage = 'One second passed!';
setTimeout(function() {
    alert(alertMessage);
}, 1000);
```

In many cases, using anonymous callbacks is a more convenient way of programming, since it results in shorter code and also reduces the readability noise, which is a result of defining several different named functions that are used only once.

Setting callbacks as object properties

A small variation of the above definition also exists, where the callback function is assigned to a property of an object instead of being passed as an argument of a method invocation. This is commonly used in cases where there are several different actions that need to take place during or after a method invocation is completed:

```
var c = new Countdown();

c.onProgress = function(progressStatus) { /*...*/ };
c.onDone = function(result) {  /*...*/ };
c.onError = function(error) {  /*...*/ };

c.start();
```

Another use case of the above variant is to add handlers on objects that have already been instantiated and initialized. A good example of this case is the way we set up a result handler for simple (non-jQuery) AJAX calls:

```
var r = new XMLHttpRequest();
r.open('GET', 'data.json', true);
r.onreadystatechange = function() {
    if (r.readyState != 4 || r.status != 200) {
        return;
    }
    alert(r.responseText);
};
r.send();
```

In the preceding code, we set an anonymous function on the `onreadystatechange` property of the XMLHttpRequest object. This function acts as a callback and is invoked every time there is a state change on the ongoing request. Inside our callback, we check whether the request has completed with a successful HTTP status code and display an alert with the response body. Like in this example, where we initiate the AJAX call by invoking the `send()` method without passing any arguments, it is common for APIs that use this variant to lead to minimal ways of invoking their methods.

Using callbacks in jQuery applications

Perhaps the most common way in which callbacks are used in jQuery applications is for event handling. This is logical since the first thing that every interactive application should do is handle and respond to user actions. As we saw in earlier chapters, one of the most convenient ways to attach event handlers to elements is by using jQuery's `$.fn.on()` method.

Another common place where callbacks are used in jQuery is for AJAX requests, where the `$.ajax()` method has the central role. Moreover, the jQuery library also provides several other convenient methods to make AJAX requests that are focused on the most common use cases. Since all these methods are executed asynchronously, they also accept a callback as a parameter, as a way to make the retrieved data available back to the context that initiated the AJAX request. One of these convenient methods is `$.getJSON()`, which is a wrapper around `$.ajax()`, and is used as a better matching API to execute AJAX requests that intend to retrieve JSON responses.

Other widely used jQuery APIs accepting callbacks are as follows:

- The effects-related jQuery methods such as `$.animate()`
- The `$(document).ready()` method

Let's now continue by demonstrating a code example where all the above methods are used.

```
$(document).ready(function() {
  $('#fetchButton').on('click', function() {
    $.getJSON('AjaxContent.json', function(json) {
      console.log('done loading new content');

      $('#newContent').css({ 'display': 'none' })
        .text(json.data)
        .slideDown(function() {
          console.log('done displaying new content');
        });
    });
  });
});
```

The preceding code firstly delays its execution until the DOM tree of the page has been fully loaded and then adds an Observer for clicks on the <button> with ID fetchButton by using the jQuery's $.fn.on() method. Whenever the click event is fired, the provided callback will be invoked and initiate an AJAX call to fetch the AjaxContent.json file. For the needs of this example, we are using a simple JSON file, like the following:

```
{ "data": "I'm the text content fetched by an AJAX call!" }
```

When the response is received and the JSON is parsed successfully, the callback is invoked with the parsed object as a parameter. Finally, the callback itself locates the page element with the ID newContent in the page, hides it, and then sets the data field of the retrieved JSON as its text content. Right after this, we use the jQuery $.fn.slideDown() method that makes the newly set page content appear, by progressively increasing its height. Finally, after the animation is complete, we write a log message to the browser console.

Further documentation regarding jQuery's $.ajax(), $.getJSON(), and $.fn.slideDown() methods can be found at http://api.jquery.com/jQuery.ajax/, http://api.jquery.com/jQuery.getJSON/, and http://api.jquery.com/slideDown/.

Keep in mind that the $.getJSON() method might not work in some browsers when the page is loaded through the filesystem, but works as intended when served using any web server such as Apache, IIS, or nginx.

Writing methods that accept callbacks

When writing a function that utilizes one or more asynchronous APIs, that also dictates that the resulting function will be asynchronous by definition. In that case, it is obvious that simply returning a result value is not an option, since the result will probably be available after the function invocation has already finished.

The easiest solution for asynchronous implementations is to use a callback as a parameter of your function, which, as we discussed earlier, is hassle-free in JavaScript. As an example, we will create an asynchronous function that generates a random number of a specified range:

```
function getRandomNumberAsync (max, callbackFn) {
    var runFor = 1000 + Math.random() * 1000;
    setTimeout(function() {
        var result = Math.random() * max;
        callbackFn(result);
    }, runFor);
}
```

The `getRandomNumberAsync()` function accepts its `max` argument as the numeric upper bound for the generated random number and also a callback function that it will invoke with the generated result. It uses `setTimeout()` to emulate an asynchronous calculation that ranges from 1000 to 2000 milliseconds. For the generation of the result, it uses the `Math.random()` method, multiplying it with the maximum allowed value, and finally invokes the provided callback with it. A simple way to invoke this function will look as follows:

```
getRandomNumberAsync(10, function(number) {
    console.log(number); // returns a number between 0 and 10
});
```

Even though the above example uses `setTimeout()` to emulate asynchronous processing, the implementation principles remain the same regardless of the asynchronous API(s) that is used. For example, we can rewrite the above function to retrieve its result through an AJAX call:

```
function getRandomNumberWS (max, callbackFn, errorFn) {
  $.ajax({
    url: 'https://qrng.anu.edu.au/API/jsonI.php?length=1&type=uint16',
    dataType: 'json',
    success: function(json) {
      var result = json.data[0] / 65535 * max;
      callbackFn(result);
    },
```

```
        error: errorFn
    });
}
```

The preceding implementation uses the $.ajax() method that is invoked with an object parameter, enclosing all the options of the request. Except for the URL for the request, the object also defines the expected dataType of the result and the success and error callbacks, which are wired with the respective parameters of our function.

Perhaps the only extra concern that the preceding code has to resolve is how to handle errors inside the success callback so that the caller of the function can be notified in case something goes wrong during the creation of the result. For example, the AJAX request might return an empty object. Adding proper handling for such cases is left as an exercise for the reader, after reading the rest of this chapter.

> The Australian National University (ANU) provides free, truly random, numbers to the public, through their REST Web Service. For more information, you can visit http://qrng.anu.edu.au/API/api-demo.php.

Orchestrating callbacks

We will now continue by analyzing some patterns that are commonly used to control the execution flow when dealing with asynchronous methods that accept callbacks.

Queuing in order execution

As our first example, we will create a function that demonstrates how we can queue the execution of several asynchronous tasks:

```
function getThreeRandomNumbers(callbackFn, errorFn) {
    var results = [];
    getRandomNumberAsync(10, function(number) {
        results.push(number);

        getRandomNumberAsync(10, function(number) {
            results.push(number);

            getRandomNumberWS(10, function(number) {
                results.push(number);
                callbackFn(results);
            }, function (error) {
```

```
                    errorFn(error);
                });
            });
        });
    }
```

In the preceding implementation, our function creates a queue of three random number generations. The first two random numbers are generated from our sample `setTimeout()` implementation and the third is retrieved from the aforementioned web service though an AJAX call. In this example, all the numbers are gathered in the `result` array, which is passed as an invocation parameter to the `callbackFn` after all the asynchronous tasks have completed.

The preceding implementation is quite straightforward and just applies the simple principles of the Callback Pattern repeatedly. For every extra or queued asynchronous task, we just need to nest its invocation inside the callback of the task that it depends on. Keep in mind that, in different use cases, we might only care to return the result of the final task and have the results of the intermediate steps be propagated as arguments for each subsequent asynchronous call.

Avoiding the Callback Hell anti-pattern

Even though writing code as shown in the above example is easy, when applied to large and complex implementations, it can lead to bad readability. The triangular shape that is created by the white-spaces in front of our code and the stacking of several `});` near its end, are the two signs that our code might lead to an anti-pattern known as **Callback Hell**.

 For more information, you can visit `http://callbackhell.com/`.

A way to avoid this anti-pattern is to unfold the nested callbacks, by creating separate named functions at the same level with the asynchronous task that they are used. After applying this simple tip to the above example, the resulting code looks a lot cleaner:

```
function getThreeRandomNumbers(callbackFn, errorFn) {
    var results = [];

    getRandomNumberAsync(10, function(number) { // task 1
        results.push(number);
        task2();
    });
```

```
function task2 () {
    getRandomNumberAsync(10, function(number) {
        results.push(number);
        task3();
    });
}

function task3 () {
    getRandomNumberWS(10, function(number) {
        results.push(number);
        callbackFn(results);
    }, errorFn);
}
}
```

As you can see, the resulting code surely does not remind us of the characteristics of the Callback Hell anti-pattern. On the other hand, it now needs more lines of code for its implementation, mostly used for the additional function declarations `function taskX () { }` that are now required.

 A middle ground solution between the above two approaches is to organize the related parts of such asynchronous execution queues in small and manageable functions.

Running concurrently

Even though JavaScript in web browsers is single-threaded, making independent asynchronous tasks run concurrently can make our applications work faster. As an example, we will rewrite the preceding implementation to fetch all three random numbers in parallel, which can make the result to be retrieved a lot faster than before:

```
function getRandomNumbersConcurent(callbackFn, errorFn) {
    var results = [];
    var resultCount = 0;
    var n = 3;

    function gatherResult (resultPos) {
        return function (result) {
            results[resultPos] = result;
            resultCount++;
            if (resultCount === n) {
                callbackFn(results);
            }
```

```
                };
        }

        getRandomNumberAsync(10, gatherResult(0));
        getRandomNumberAsync(10, gatherResult(1));
        getRandomNumberWS(10, gatherResult(2), errorFn);
    }
```

In the preceding code, we defined the `gatherResult()` helper function, which returns an anonymous function that is used as a callback for our random number generators. The returned callback function uses the `resultPos` parameter as the index of the array where it will store the generated or retrieved random number. Additionally, it tracks how many times it has been invoked, as a way to know whether all three concurrent tasks have ended. Finally, right after the third and final invocation of the callback, the `callbackFn` function is invoked with the `results` array as a parameter.

Another great application of this technique, other than AJAX calls, is to access data stored in **IndexedDB**. Retrieving many values from the database concurrently can lead to performance gains, since the data retrievals can execute in parallel without blocking each other.

For more information on IndexedDB, you can visit `https://developer.mozilla.org/en-US/docs/Web/API/IndexedDB_API/Using_IndexedDB`.

Introducing the concept of Promises

Promises, also known as Futures, are described by Computer Science as specialized objects that are used for synchronization of asynchronous, concurrent, or parallel procedures. They are also used as proxies to propagate the result of a task when its generation completes. This way, a Promise object is like a contract where an operation will eventually complete its execution, and anyone having a reference to this contract can declare their interest to be notified about the result.

Since they were introduced to JavaScript developers, as part of several libraries, they revolutionized the way we use asynchronous functions and compose them in implementation with complex synchronization schemes. This way, web developers can create more flexible, scalable, and readable implementations, making method invocations with callbacks look like a primitive pattern and effectively eliminating the Callback Hell situations.

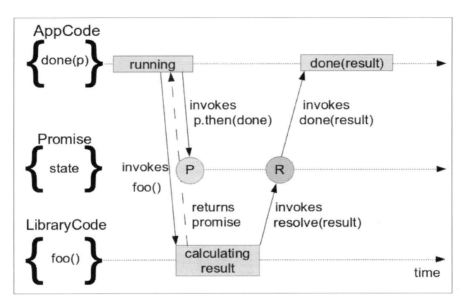

One of the key concepts of Promises is that asynchronous methods return an object that represents their eventual result. Every Promise has an internal state that initially starts as Pending. This internal state can change only once, from Pending to either Resolved or Rejected, by using one of the resolve() or reject() methods that every implementation provides. These methods can be invoked only to change the state of a Pending Promise; in most cases, they are intended to be used only by the original creator of the Promise object and not be available to its consumers. The resolve() method can be invoked with the result of the operation as a single parameter, while the reject() method is usually invoked with the Error that caused the Promise object to get Rejected.

Another key concept of Promises is the existence of a `then()` method, giving them the characterization of the "thenable", as a general term to describe promises among all the different implementations. Every Promise object exposes a `then()` method that is used by a caller in order to provide the function(s) that will be invoked when the Promise is settled (Resolved or Rejected). The `then()` method can be invoked with two functions as parameters, where the first is invoked in case the Promise gets Resolved, while the second is invoked when it is Rejected. The first argument is commonly referred to as the `onFulfilled()` callback, while the second is referred to as the `onRejected()`.

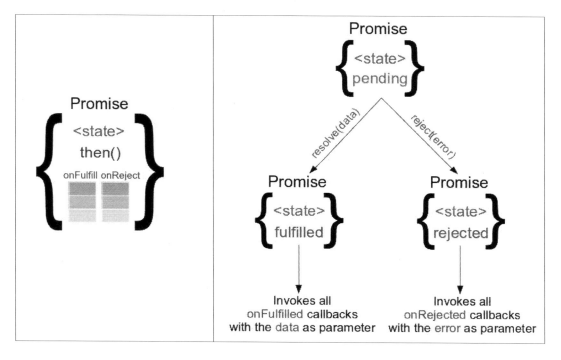

Every Promise preserves two internal list containing all the `onFulfilled()` and `onRejected()` callback functions that are passed as arguments to the `then()` method. The `then()` method can be invoked several times for each Promise, adding new entries to the appropriate internal list, as far as the respective parameter is actually a function. When a Promise eventually gets Resolved or Rejected, it iterates over the appropriate list of callbacks and invokes them in order. Moreover, from the point that a Promise gets settled and after, every further usage of the `then()` method has, as a result, the immediate invocation of the appropriate provided callback.

Based on its characteristics, a Promise can be likened to a Broker from the Publish/Subscribe Pattern to some degree. Their key differences include the facts that it can only be used for a single Publish and that the Subscribers get notified of the result even if they expressed their interest after the Publish took place.

Using Promises

As we said earlier, the concept of Promises revolutionized programming of asynchronous tasks in JavaScript and, for a long time, they were the new big thing that everyone was enthusiastic about. At that time, many specialized libraries appeared where each one provided an implementation of Promises with slight differences to each other. Moreover, Promise implementations became available as part of utility libraries such as jQuery and web frameworks such as AngularJS and EmberJS. At that time, the "CommonJS Promises/A" specification made its appearance as a reference point and was the first attempt to define how Promises should actually work across all implementations.

For more information on the "CommonJS Promises/A" specification, you can visit http://wiki.commonjs.org/wiki/Promises/A.

Using the jQuery Promise API

A Promise-based API first appeared in the jQuery library in v1.5, based on the "CommonJS Promises/A" design. This implementation introduced the additional concept of the Deferred object, which works like a **Promise Factory**. The Deferred objects expose a superset of the methods that Promises provide, where the additional methods can be used to do manipulations to the state of its internal Promise. Additionally, the Deferred object exposes a promise() method and returns the actual Promise object, which does not expose any way to manipulate its internal state and just exposes observation methods such as then().

In other words:

- Only code that has a reference to a Deferred object can actually change the internal state of its Promise, by either resolving or rejecting it.

- Any piece of code that has a reference to a Promise object can't change its state but just observe for its state to change.

For more information on jQuery's Deferred object, you can visit
http://api.jquery.com/jQuery.Deferred/.

As a simple example of jQuery's Deferred object, let's see how we can rewrite the
getRandomNumberAsync() function that we saw earlier in this chapter, to use
Promises instead of Callbacks:

```
function getRandomNumberAsync (max) {
    var d = $.Deferred();
    var runFor = 1000 + Math.random() * 1000;
    setTimeout(function() {
        var result = Math.random() * max;
        d.resolve(result);
    }, runFor);
    return d.promise();
}

getRandomNumberAsync(10).then(function(number) {
    console.log(number); // returns a number between 0 and 10
});
```

Our target is to make an asynchronous function that returns a Promise that is
eventually resolved to the resulting random number. At first, a new Deferred object
is created and then the respective Promise object is returned, by using the promise()
method of the Deferred. When the asynchronous generation of the result is complete,
our method uses the resolve() method of the Deferred object to set the final state of
the Promise that was returned earlier.

The caller of our function uses the then() method of the returned Promise, to attach
a callback that will be invoked with the result as a parameter as soon as the Promise
gets Resolved. Moreover, a second callback can also be passed in order to get notified
in case the Promise gets Rejected. An important thing to notice is that, by following
the above pattern where functions always return Promises and never the actual
Deferred objects, we can be sure that only the creator of the Deferred object can
change the state of the Promise.

Using Promises/A+

After some time of hands-on experimentation with CommonJS Promises/A, the community identified some of their limitations and also recommended some ways to improve them. The result was the creation of the Promises/A+ specification, as a way to improve the existing specification and also as a second attempt to unify the various available implementations. The most important parts of the new specification focused on how chaining Promises should work, making them even more useful and convenient to work with.

 For more information on the Promises/A+ specification, you can visit `https://promisesaplus.com/`.

Finally, the Promises/A+ specification was published as part of the 6th version of JavaScript, commonly referred as ES6, that was released as a standard on June, 2015. As a result, Promises/A+ started to be implemented natively in browsers, removing the need to use custom third-party libraries and pushing most of the existing libraries to upgrade their semantics. As of writing of this book, native Promises/A+ compliant implementations have been available in most modern browsers, except for IE11, making them available out-of-the-box to more than 65% of web users.

 For more information on the adoption of A+ Promises in browsers, you can visit `http://caniuse.com/#feat=promises`.

A rewrite of the `getRandomNumberAsync()` function using the now natively implemented ES6 A+ Promises will look as follows:

```
function getRandomNumberAsync (max) {
    return new Promise(function (resolve, reject) {
        var runFor = 1000 + Math.random() * 1000;
        setTimeout(function() {
            var result = Math.random() * max;
            resolve(result);
        }, runFor);
    });
}

getRandomNumberAsync(10).then(function(number) {
    console.log(number); // returns a number between 0 and 10
});
```

As you can see, ES6 / A+ Promises are created by using the Promise constructor function with the `new` keyword. The constructor is invoked with a function as a parameter, which makes a closure that has access to both the variables of the context that the Promise is created, but also gets access to the `resolve()` and `reject()` functions as parameters, which is the only way to change the state of the newly created Promise. After the `setTimeout()` function fires its callback, the `resolve()` function is invoked with the generated random number as a parameter, changing the state of the Promise object to Fulfilled. Finally, the caller of our function uses the `then()` method of the returned Promise in exactly the same way as we saw in the earlier implementation that was using jQuery.

Comparing jQuery and A+ Promises

We will now have an in-depth step-by-step analysis of the core concepts of the jQuery and A+ Promise APIs, by also doing a side-by-side code comparison of the two. This can be a great asset to have, since you will also be able to use it as a reference while the implementations of Promises are gradually adapting to the ES6 A+ specification.

The need to understand from the beginning how the two variants differ seems even greater, since the jQuery team has already announced that Version 3.0 of the library will have Promises/A+ compliant implementation. Specifically, as of writing this book, the first beta version is already out, making the time that the migration will happen to appear even closer.

 For more information on jQuery v3.0 A+ Promises implementation, you can visit http://blog.jquery.com/2016/01/14/jquery-3-0-beta-released/.

One of the most obvious differences between the two implementations is the way that new Promises are created. As we saw, jQuery uses the `$.Deferred()` function like a factory of a more complex object that provides direct access to the state of the Promise and eventually extracts the actual Promise using a separate method. On the other hand, A+ Promises use the `new` keyword and a function as a parameter, which will be invoked by the runtime with the `resolve()` and `reject()` functions as parameters:

```
var d = $.Deferred();
setTimeout(function() {
    d.resolve(7);
}, 2000);
var p = d.promise(); // jQuery Promise
```

```
var p = new Promise(function(resolve, reject) { // Promises/A+
    setTimeout(function() {
        resolve(7);
    }, 2000);
});
```

Moreover, jQuery also provides another way to create Promises that look more like the way that A+ Promises work. In this case, `$.Deferred()` can be invoked with a function as an argument that receives the Deferred object as a parameter:

```
var d = $.Deferred(function (deferred) {
    setTimeout(function() {
        deferred.resolve(7);
    }, 2000);
});
var p = d.promise();
```

As we discussed earlier, the second possible outcome of a Promise is to be Rejected, a feature that nicely pairs with the classical exceptions of JavaScript in synchronous programming. Rejecting a Promise is commonly used for cases where an error occurs during the processing of the result, or in situations where the result is not valid. While ES6 Promises provide a `reject()` function as an argument to the function passed to its constructor, in jQuery's implementation a `reject()` method is simply exposed on the Deferred object itself.

```
var p = $.Deferred(function (deferred) {
    deferred.reject(new Error('Something happened!'));
}).promise();

var p = new Promise(function(resolve, reject) {
    reject(new Error('Something happened!'));
});
```

In both the implementations, the result of a Promise can be retrieved using the `then()` method, which can be invoked with two functions as arguments, one to handle the case that the Promise gets Fulfilled and one for the case where it is Rejected:

```
p.then(function(result) { // works the same in jQuery & ES6
    console.log(result);
}, function(error) {
    console.error('An error occurred: ', error);
});
```

Both implementations also provide convenient methods to handle the case where the Promise gets Rejected, but with different method names. Instead of using `p.then(null, fn)`, ES6 Promises provide the `catch()` method that nicely pairs with the try...catch JavaScript expression, while jQuery's implementation provides, for the same purpose, the `fail()` method:

```
p.fail(function(error) { // jQuery
    console.error(error);
});

p.catch(function(error) { // ES6
    console.error(error);
});
```

Moreover, as a jQuery exclusive feature, jQuery Promises also expose a `done()` and an `always()` method. The callbacks provided to `done()` are invoked when the Promise gets Fulfilled and is equivalent to using the `then()` method with a single parameter, while the callbacks of the `always()` method are invoked when the promise gets settled in both possible outcomes.

> For more information on `done()` and `always()`, you can visit `http://api.jquery.com/deferred.done` and `http://api.jquery.com/deferred.always`.

Finally, both implementations provide an easy way to directly create Promises that are already Resolved or Rejected. This can be useful as a starting value to implement complex synchronization schemes or as an easy way to make synchronous functions to operate like asynchronous ones:

```
var pResolved = $.Deferred().resolve(7).promise(); // jQuery
var pRejected = $.Deferred().reject(new Error('Something happened!'))
    .promise();

var pResolved = Promise.resolve(7); // ES6
var pRejected = Promise.reject(new Error('Something happened!'));
```

Advanced concepts

Another key concept of Promises that makes them unique and greatly increases their usefulness is the ability to easily create compositions of several Promises that in turn are Promises themselves. Composition is available in two forms, serial composition that chains Promises together and parallel composition that uses special methods to join the resolution of concurrent Promises into a new one. As we saw earlier in this chapter, implementing such synchronization schemes can be hard to implement with the traditional callback approach. Promises, on the other hand, try to solve this problem in a more convenient and readable way.

Chaining Promises

Every invocation of the `then()` method returns a new Promise, whose both final status and result depends on the Promise that the `then()` method was called on, but is also subject to the value returned by the attached callbacks. This allows us to chain calls of the `then()` method, enabling us to compose Promises by serially joining them. This way, we can easily orchestrate both asynchronous and synchronous code, where each chaining step propagates its result to the next one and allows us to construct the final result in a readable and declarative way.

Let's now proceed to analyzing all the different ways that chaining of calls to the `then()` method works. Since we will be focusing on the concepts of Promise composition by chaining, which works the same as jQuery and ES6 Promises, let's suppose that there is a `p` variable that is holding a Promise object created by either of the following lines of code:

```
var p = $.Deferred().resolve(7).promise();
//or
var p = Promise.resolve(7);
```

The simplest use case that demonstrates the power of chaining is when the invoked callback returns a (non-promise) value. The newly created Promise uses the returned value as its result, while preserving the same state as the Promise that the `then()` method was called on:

```
p.then(function(x) { // works the same in jQuery & ES6
    console.log(x); // logs 7
    return x * 3;
}).then(function(x) {
    console.log(x); // logs 21
});
```

A special case to have in mind is that functions that do not return anything as a result are handled like returning `undefined`. This essentially removes the result value from the newly returned Promise, which now only preserves the parent settlement status:

```
p.then(function(x) { // works the same in jQuery & ES6
    console.log(x); // logs 7
}).then(function(x) {
    console.log(x); // logs undefined
});
```

In the case where the invoked callback returns another Promise, its state and result are used for the Promise returned by the `then()` method:

```
p.then(function(x) { // for jQuery Promises
    console.log(x); // logs 7
    var d2 = $.Deferred();
    setTimeout(function() {
        d2.resolve(x*3);
    }, 2000);
    return d2.promise();
}).then(function(x) {
    console.log(x); // logs 21
});

p.then(function(x) { // for the A+ Promises
    console.log(x); // logs 7
    return new Promise(function(resolve) {
        setTimeout(function() {
            resolve(x*3);
        }, 2000);
    });
}).then(function(x) {
    console.log(x); // logs 21
});
```

The preceding code samples demonstrate the implementations for both the jQuery and A+ Promises, and both have equivalent results. In both cases, 7 is logged into the console from the first `then()` method invocation and a new Promise is then returned that will be Resolved at a later time using `setTimeout()`. After 2000 milliseconds, that `setTimeout()` will fire its callback, the returned Promise will be Resolved with 21 as a value and, at that point, 21 will also be logged into the console.

One extra thing to note is the case where the original Promise gets settled and there is no appropriate callback provided to the chained `then()` method. In this case, the newly created Promise settles to the same state and result, as the Promise where the `then()` method was called on:

```
p.then(null, function (error) { // works the same in jQuery & ES6
    console.error('An error happened!');
    // does not run, since the promise is resolved
}).then(function(x) {
    console.log(x); // logs 7
});
```

In the preceding example, the callback with the `console.error` statement that is passed as the second argument of the `then()` method, does not get invoked since the Promise is resolved with 7 as its value. As a result, the callback of the chain eventually receives a new Promise, which is also resolved with 7 as its value and logs that in the console. Something to have in mind in order to deeply understand how chaining of Promises works, is that `p != p.then()` in all cases.

Handling thrown errors

The final concept of chaining defines the case where exceptions are thrown during the invocation of a `then()` callback. The Promise/A+ specification defined that the newly created Promise is Rejected and that its result is the `Error` that was thrown. Moreover, the Rejection will bubble through the entire chain of Promises, enabling us to be notified about any error in the chain only defining the error handling once, near to the end of the chain.

Unfortunately, this is not consistent in the implementation of the latest stable version of jQuery, which as of the writing of this book is v2.2.0:

```
$.Deferred().resolve().promise().then(function() {
    throw new Error('Something happened!');
    // the execution stops here
}).then(null, function(x) {
    console.log(x); // nothing gets printed
});

$.Deferred().resolve().promise().then(function() {
    try { // this is a workaround
        throw new Error('Something happened!');
    } catch (e) {
        return $.Deferred().reject(e).promise();
    }
}).then(function(){
    console.log('Success'); // not printed
}).then(null, function(x) { // almost equivalent to .fail()
    console.log(x); // logs 'Something happened!''
});

Promise.resolve().then(function() {
    throw new Error('Something happened!');
}).then(function(){
    console.log('Success'); // not printed
}).then(null, function(x) { // equivalent to .catch()
    console.log(x); // logs 'Something happened!''
});
```

In the first case, the exception that is thrown stops the execution of the Promise chain. The only way around it is probably explicitly adding a try...catch statement inside the callback that is passed to the `then()` method, as shown in the second case that is demonstrated.

Joining Promises

The other way of orchestrating Promises that run concurrently is by composing them together. As an example, let's suppose the existence of two Promises, p1 and p2, that get resolved with 7 and 11 as their values, after 2000 and 3000 milliseconds, respectively. Since these two Promises are executed concurrently, the composed Promise will only need 3000 milliseconds to get Resolved, as it is the greater of the two durations:

```
// jQuery
$.when(p1, p2).then(function(result1, result2) {
    console.log('p1', result1); // logs 7
    console.log('p2', result2); // logs 11
    // this can be used to make our code look like A+
    var results = arguments;
});
```

```
// A+
Promise.all([p1, p2]).then(function(results) {
    console.log('p1', results[0]); // logs 7
    console.log('p2', results[1]); // logs 11
});
```

Both Promise APIs provide a specialized function that allows us to easily create Promise compositions and also retrieve the individual results of the composition. A composed Promise gets Resolved when all its parts get Resolved, while it gets Rejected when any one of its parts gets Rejected. Unfortunately, the two Promise APIs differ, not only by the name of the functions, but also by the way they are invoked and the way they provide their results.

The jQuery implementation provides the `$.when()` method that can be invoked with any number of arguments that we want to be composed. By using the `then()` method on a composed jQuery Promise, we can get notified when the composition gets settled as a whole and also access each individual result as arguments of our callback.

On the other hand, the A+ Promises specification provides us the `Promise.all()` method that is invoked with an array as its single parameter that contains all the Promises that we want to get composed. The returned composed Promise does not differ at all from the Promises that we have seen so far and the callback of the `then()` method is invoked with an array as its parameter, which contains all the results of the Promises that are part of the composition.

How jQuery uses Promises

At the time that jQuery added an implementation of Promises to its API, it also started to expose it through other asynchronous methods of its API. Perhaps the most well-known example of this kind is the method of the `$.ajax()` family that returns a jqXHR object, which is a specialized Promise object that also provides some extra methods related to the AJAX request.

> For more information on the jQuery's `$.ajax()` method and the jqXHR object, you can visit `http://api.jquery.com/jQuery.ajax/#jqXHR`. The jQuery team also decided to change the implementation of several internal parts of the library to use Promises, in order to improve their implementations. First of all, the `$.ready()` method is implemented using Promises so that the provided callbacks fire even if the page has already been loaded a long time before its invocation. Also, some of the complex animations that jQuery provides use Promises internally as the preferred way to synchronize the execution of the sequential parts of the animation queue.

Transforming Promises to other types

Developing by using several different JavaScript libraries often makes many Promise implementations available to our projects that unfortunately tend to have different levels of compliance to the reference Promises specification. Composing Promises returned by the methods of different libraries can often lead to problems that are hard to track and resolve, as a result of their implementation inconsistencies.

In order to avoid confusions in such situations, it isn't considered a good practice to transform all the Promises to a single type before attempting to compose them. The suggested type for such situations is the Promises/A+ specification, since not only is it widely accepted by the community but it is also part of the newly released version of JavaScript (the ES6 language specification) that is already natively implemented in many browsers.

Transforming to Promises/A+

For example, let's see how a jQuery Promise can be transformed to an A+ Promise that is available in most recent browsers:

```
var jqueryPromise = $.Deferred().resolve('I will be A+ compliant')
    .promise();
var p = Promise.resolve(jqueryPromise);
p.then(function(result) {
    console.log(result);
});
```

In the preceding example, the `Promise.resolve()` method detects that it has been invoked with a "thenable" and that the newly created A+ Promise that is returned binds its status and result to those of the provided jQuery Promise. This is essentially equivalent to doing something as follows:

```
var p = new Promise(function (resolve, reject) {
    jqueryPromise.then(resolve, reject);
});
```

Of course, this is not limited to Promises that are created by direct invocations of the `$.Deferred()` method. The above technique can also be used to transform Promises that are returned by any jQuery method. For example, this is how it can be used with the `$.getJSON()` method:

```
var aPlusAjaxPromise = Promise.resolve($.getJSON('AjaxContent.json'));
aPlusAjaxPromise.then(function(result) {
    console.log(result);
});
```

Transforming to jQuery Promises

Even though I would generally not recommend this, it is also possible to transform any Promise to a jQuery variant. The newly created jQuery Promise receives all the extra functionalities that jQuery provides, but the transformation is not as straightforward as the previous one:

```
var aPromise = Promise.resolve('I will be a jQuery Promise');
var p = $.Deferred(function (deferred) {
    aPromise.then(function(result) {
        return deferred.resolve(result);
    }, function(error) {
        return deferred.reject(error);
    });
```

```
}).promise();
p.then(function(result) {
    console.log(result);
});
```

You should only use the preceding technique in cases where you need to extend a big web application that is already implemented using jQuery Promises. On the other hand, you should also consider upgrading such implementations, since the jQuery team has already announced that Version 3.0 of the library will have Promises/A+ compliant implementation.

 For more information on jQuery v3.0 A+ Promises implementation, you can visit `http://blog.jquery.com/2016/01/14/ jquery-3-0-beta-released/`.

Summarizing the benefits of Promises

Overall, the benefits of using Promises over plain Callbacks include:

- Having a unified way to handle the result of asynchronous invocations
- Having predictable invocation parameters for the used callbacks
- The ability to attach multiple handlers for each outcome of the Promise
- The guarantee that the appropriate attached handlers will execute even if the Promise has already been Resolved (or Rejected)
- The ability to chain asynchronous operations, making them run in order
- The ability to easily create compositions of asynchronous operations, making them run concurrently
- The convenient way of handling errors in Promise chains

Using a method that returns a Promise removes the need to directly pass functions of one context to another as an invocation argument and the question regarding which parameters are used as the success and the error Callbacks. Moreover, we already know to some degree how to retrieve the result of any operation that returns a Promise, by using the `then()` method, even before reading the documentation about the method's invocation parameters.

Less parameters often means less complexity, smaller documentation, and less searching every time we want to do a method invocation. Even better, there is a good chance that there will only be a single or a few parameters, making the invocation more sensible and readable. The implementation of asynchronous methods also becomes less complex, since there is no longer the need to accept callback functions as an extra argument or having to properly invoke them with the result.

Summary

In this chapter, we analyzed the development patterns that are used to program asynchronous and concurrent procedures. We also learned how to use them to efficiently orchestrate the execution of asynchronous procedures that run either in order or parallel to each other.

At first, we had a refresher on how Callbacks are used in JavaScript programming and how they are an integral part of web development. We analyzed their benefits and limitations when used in large and complex implementations.

Right after this, we were introduced to the concepts of Promises. We learned how jQuery's Deferred and Promise APIs work and how they differ from ES6 Promises. We also saw where and how they are used internally by jQuery itself, as an example of how they can lead to more readable code and simplify such complex implementations.

In the next chapter, we will proceed to learning how to design, create, and use Mock Objects and Mock Services in our applications. We will analyze the characteristics that a proper Mock Object should have and understand how they can be used as representative use cases and even as test cases for our code.

8
Mock Object Pattern

In this chapter we will showcase the Mock Object Pattern, a pattern to facilitate the development of applications without actually being part of the final implementation. We will learn how to design, create and use this industry-standard design pattern in order to coordinate and complete the development of multi-part jQuery applications faster. We will analyze the characteristics that a proper Mock Object should have and understand how they can be used as representative use cases and even as test cases for our code.

We will see how good application architecture makes it easier for us to use Mock Objects & Services by matching individual parts of the application, and also realize the benefits of using them during development. By the end of this chapter, we will be able to create Mock Objects & Services to accelerate the implementation of our application and also to get a sense of the overall functionality long before all of its parts are completed.

In this chapter, we shall:

- Introduce the Mock Object and Mock Service Patterns
- Analyze the characteristics that Mock Objects & Services should have
- Understand why they fit better with applications with good architecture
- Learn how to use them in jQuery applications as a way to drive the development and accelerate it

Introducing the Mock Object Pattern

The key concept of the Mock Object Pattern is in creating and using a dummy object that simulates the behavior of a more complex object that is (or will be) part of an implementation. The Mock Object should have the same API as the actual (or real) object, return similar results using the same data structures, and also operate in a similar manner with regards to how its methods alter its exposed state (the properties).

Mock Objects are usually created during the early development phases of an application. Their primary use case is to enable us to proceed with the development of a Module, even if it depends on others that have not yet been implemented. Mock Objects can also be described as prototypes of the data exchanged between the different parts of the implementation, acting like contracts between the developers and easing the parallel development of interdependent modules.

In the same way that the principles of the Module Pattern decouple the implementations of the different parts of an application, creating and using Mock Objects and Mock Services decouples their development.

Creating Mock Objects for every Module before starting their implementation clearly defines the data structures and APIs that will be used by the application, removing any misconceptions and enabling us to detect insufficiencies in the proposed APIs.

Defining the data structures that are required to describe a problem before starting the actual implementation allows us to focus on the needs of the application and get an idea of its overall complexity and structure.

You can always test any part of your implementation after any code change by using the Mock Objects that were created for the original implementation. You can be sure that the original use case still works by using the Mock Objects on the modified methods. This is very useful when the modified implementation is a part of a use case involving several stages.

Mock Objects are especially useful for tracing errors if the implementation of a Module has changed and caused the rest of the application to misbehave. By using the existing Mock Objects, we can easily identify the Module that diverged from the original specification. Moreover, the same Mock Objects can be used as the basis for high quality test cases since they often contain more realistic sample data, something especially useful if your team is following a Test Driven Development (TDD) paradigm.

In Test Driven Development (TDD), the developer firstly defines a test case for a use case or a new feature that needs to be added and then proceeds with its implementation by trying to satisfy the created test case. For more information, you can visit: `https://www.packtpub.com/books/content/overview-tdd`.

The Mock Object Pattern is commonly used among frontend web developers to decouple the client-side development from the web services that the backend will expose. That has led to witty comments such as:

"The web service will always be late & change suddenly, so use a Mock instead."

Summarizing all of this, the main reasons to create Mock Objects and Services include:

- The actual object or service is not yet implemented.
- The actual object is difficult to set up for a specific use case.
- We need to emulate a rare or non-deterministic behavior.
- The actual object behaves in a way that is hard to reproduce, such as network errors or UI events.

Using Mock Objects in jQuery applications

In order to demonstrate how the Mock Object Pattern can be used during the development of a multi-part application, we will extend the dashboard example, as we saw in *Chapter 4, Divide and Conquer with the Module Pattern*, in order to present thumbnails of YouTube videos from web developing conferences. The video references are grouped into four predefined categories and the related buttons will be displayed based on the current category selection, as illustrated below:

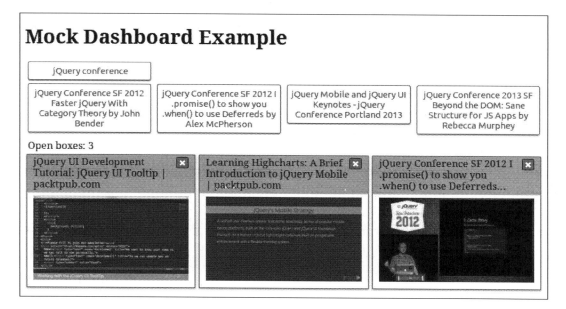

The changes that need to be introduced to the HTML and the CSS are minimal. The only extra CSS that is needed for the above implementation, when compared to the existing implementation from *Chapter 4, Divide and Conquer with the Module Pattern*, is related to the width of the thumbnails:

```
.box img {
  width: 100%;
}
```

The change in the HTML is intended to organize the `<button>` elements of each category. This change will make our implementation more straightforward since the categories and their items are no longer statically defined in the HTML but are instead created dynamically, driven by the available data.

```
<!-- … -->
<section class="dashboardCategories">
  <select id="categoriesSelector"></select>
  <div class="dashboardCategoriesList"></div>
  <div class="clear"></div>
</section>
<!-- … -->
```

In the above piece of HTML, the `<div>` element with the `dashboardCategoriesList` CSS class, will be used as a container for the grouped buttons of the different video categories. After covering the UI elements, let's now move on to the analysis of the JavaScript implementation.

Defining the actual service requirements

The video references to be displayed in our dashboard could be retrieved from various sources. For example, you could make a direct call to YouTube's client-side API or an AJAX call to a backend web service . In all of the above cases, it is considered a good practice to abstract this data retrieval mechanism into a separate module, following the code structuring recommendations of the previous chapters.

For this reason, we need to add an extra module to the existing implementation. This will be a service, responsible for providing the methods that will allow us to retrieve the most relevant videos from each category and load information for each video individually. This will be achieved by using the `searchVideos()` and `getVideo()` methods respectively.

As we have already said, one of the most important phases of each implementation, especially in case of parallel development, is the analysis and definition of the data structures to be used. Since our dashboard will be using the YouTube API, we need to create some sample data which follow its data structure rules. After inspecting the API, we end up with a sub-set of the fields that are required for our dashboard, and can proceed to create a JSON object with mock data to demonstrate the used data structure:

```
{
  "items": [{
    "id": { "videoId": "UdQbBq3APAQ" },
    "snippet": {
```

```
    "title": "jQuery UI Development Tutorial:
        jQuery UI Tooltip | packtpub.com",
    "thumbnails": {
      "default": { "url":
          "https://i.ytimg.com/vi/UdQbBq3APAQ/default.jpg" },
      "medium": { "url":
          "https://i.ytimg.com/vi/UdQbBq3APAQ/mqdefault.jpg" },
      "high": { "url":
          "https://i.ytimg.com/vi/UdQbBq3APAQ/hqdefault.jpg" }
    }
  }
}
}/*,...*/]
}
```

 For more information about the YouTube API, you can visit: `https://developers.google.com/youtube/v3/getting-started`.

Our service provides two core methods, one for searching for videos in a specified category and one for retrieving information about a specific video. The structure of the sample object is used for the search method to retrieve a set of relevant items, while the method for retrieving information for a single video uses the data structure of each individual item. The resulting implementation for the video information retrieval is in a separate module named `videoService`, which will be available on the `dashboard.videoService` namespace, and our HTML would contain a `<script>` reference like the following:

```
<script type="text/javascript" src="dashboard.videoservice.js">
</script>
```

Implementing a Mock Service

Changing the `<script>` references of the service implementation with the Mock Service and vice versa should leave us with a working application, helping us progress and test the rest of the implementation before the actual implementation of the video service is finished. As a result, the Mock Service needs to use the same `dashboard.videoService` namespace, but its implementation should be in a differently named file such as `dashboard.videoservicemock.js` that simply adds the "mock" suffix.

As we have already mentioned, it is a good practice to place all our mock data under a single variable. Moreover, if there are a lot of Mocked Objects, it is common to place them in a different file altogether, with a nested namespace. In our case, the file with the mock data is named `dashboard.videoservicemock.mockdata.js` and its namespace is `dashboard.videoService.mockData`, while exposing the `searches` and `videos` properties that will be used by the two core methods of our Mock Service.

Even though the implementations of Mock Services should be simple, they have their own complexity since they need to provide the same methods as the target implementations, accept the same arguments, and look as if they are operating in the exact same way. For example, in our case, the video retrieval service needs to be asynchronous and its implementation needs to return Promises:

```javascript
(function() { // dashboard.videoservicemock.js
    'use strict';

    dashboard.videoService = dashboard.videoService || {};

    dashboard.videoService.searchVideos = function(searchKeywords) {
        return $.Deferred(function(deferred) {
            var searches =
                dashboard.videoService.mockData.searches;
            for (var i = 0; i < searches.length; i++) {
                if (searches[i].keywords === searchKeywords) {
                    // return the first matching search results
                    deferred.resolve(searches[i].data);
                    return;
                }
            }
            deferred.reject('Not found!');
        }).promise();
    };


    dashboard.videoService.getVideo = function(videoTitle) {
        return $.Deferred(function(deferred) {
            var videos =
                dashboard.videoService.mockData.allVideos;
            for (var i = 0; i < videos.length; i++) {
                if (videos[i].snippet.title === videoTitle) {
                    // return the first matching item
                    deferred.resolve(videos[i]);
```

```
                    return;
                }
            }
            deferred.reject('Not found!');
        }).promise();
    };

    var videoBaseUrl = 'https://www.youtube.com/watch?v=';
    dashboard.videoService.getVideoUrl = function(videoId) {
        return videoBaseUrl + videoId;
    };
})();
```

As shown in the Mock Service implementation above, the `searchVideos()` and `getVideo()` methods, are iterating over the arrays with the mock data and return a Promise that is either Resolved with an appropriate Mock Object or Rejected when such an object is not found. Finally, you can see below the code for the sub-module containing the Mock Objects, following the data structure that we described earlier. Note that we store the Mock Objects of all categories in the `allVideos` property in order to make searching with the mock `getVideo()` method simpler.

```
(function() { // dashboard.videoservicemock.mockdata.js
    'use strict';

    dashboard.videoService.mockData =
        dashboard.videoService.mockData || {};

    dashboard.videoService.mockData.searches = [{
        keywords: 'jQuery conference',
        data: {
            "items": [/*...*/]
        }
    }/*,...*/];

    var allVideos = [];
    var searches = dashboard.videoService.mockData.searches;
    for (var i = 0; i < searches.length; i++) {
        allVideos = allVideos.concat(searches[i].data.items);
    }

    dashboard.videoService.mockData.allVideos = allVideos;
})();
```

Experimenting with the implementation of some Mock Services will get you familiar with their common implementation patterns in a very short period of time. Beyond that, you will be able to easily create Mock Objects and Services, helping you design the APIs of your applications, try them out by using the mocks and finally settle on the best matching methods and data structures for each use case.

Using the jQuery Mockjax library

The Mockjax jQuery Plugin library (available at `https://github.com/jakerella/jquery-mockjax`) focuses on providing a simple way of mocking or simulating AJAX requests and responses. This reduces the code needed to fully implement your own Mock Services, if all that you need is to intercept an AJAX request to a web service and return a Mock Object instead.

Using the Mock Service

In order to add the functionality that we described earlier to the existing dashboard implementation, we need to introduce some changes to the `categories` and the `informationBox` modules, adding the code that will consume the methods of our service. As a representative example of using the newly created Mock Service, let's take a look at the implementation of the `openNew()` method, in the `informationBox` module:

```javascript
dashboard.informationBox.openNew = function(itemName) {
    var $box = $('<div class="boxsizer"><article class="box">' +
            '<header class="boxHeader">' +
                '<button class="boxCloseButton">&#10006;</button>' +
                itemName +
            '</header>' +
            '<div class="boxContent">Loading...</div>' +
        '</article></div>');
    $boxContainer.append($box);

    dashboard.videoService.getVideo(itemName).then(function(result) {
        var $a = $('<a>').attr('href',
          dashboard.videoService.getVideoUrl(result.id.videoId));
        $a.append($('<img />').attr('src',
          result.snippet.thumbnails.medium.url));
        $box.find('.boxContent').empty().append($a);
    }).fail(function() {
        $buttonContainer.html('An error occurred!');
    });
};
```

This method initially opens a new information box with a **Loading...** label as its content and uses the `dashboard.videoService.getVideo()` method to retrieve the details of the requested video asynchronously. Finally, when the returned Promise gets resolved, it replaces the **Loading...** label with an anchor containing the thumbnail of the video.

Summary

In this chapter, we learned how to design, create and use Mock Objects and Mock Services in our applications. We analyzed the characteristics that Mock Objects should have and understood how they can be used as representative use cases. We are now able to use Mock Objects & Services to accelerate the implementation of our applications and get a better sense of its overall functionality, long before all of its individual parts are completed.

In the next chapter, we will be introduced to client-side templating and learn how to generate complex HTML structures in the browser from readable templates efficiently. We will get an introduction to `Underscore.js` and `Handlebars.js`, analyze their conventions, evaluate their features and find which one better suits our taste.

9
Client-side Templating

This chapter will demonstrate some of the most widely used libraries to create complex HTML templates faster, while making our implementation easier to read and understand when compared to traditional string concatenation techniques. We will learn in more detail how to use the `Underscore.js` and `Handlebars.js` templating libraries, get a taste of their conventions, evaluate their features and find the one that best suits our taste.

By the end of this chapter, we will be able to generate complex HTML structures in the browser efficiently by using readable templates and utilizing the unique characteristics of each templating library.

In this chapter, we will:

- Discuss the benefits of using a specialized templating library
- Introduce the current trends in client-side templating, specifically the top representative of the families that use `<% %>` and `{{ }}` as their placeholders
- Introduce `Underscore.js` as an example of the family of templating engines that use `<% %>` placeholders
- Introduce `Handlebars.js` as an example of the family of templating engines that use curly braces `{{ }}` placeholders

Introducing Underscore.js

`Underscore.js` is a JavaScript library that provides a collection of utility methods that help web developers work more efficiently and focus on the actual implementation of their application rather than bothering with repetitive algorithmic problems. `Underscore.js` is, by default, accessible through the "_" identifier of the global namespace and that's exactly where its name comes from.

As with the $ identifier in jQuery, the underscore "_" identifier can also be used as a variable name in JavaScript.

One of the utility functions that it provides is the _.template() method, which provides us with a convenient way of interpolating specific values into existing template strings that follow a specific format. The _.template() method recognizes three special placeholder notations inside templates, which are used to add dynamic characteristics:

- The <%= %> notation is used as the simplest way to interpolate a value of a variable or an expression in a template.

- The <%- %> notation performs HTML escaping on a variable or expression and then interpolates it in a template.

- The <% %> notation is used to execute any valid JavaScript statement as part of the template generation.

The _.template() method accepts a template string that follows these characteristics and returns a plain JavaScript function, commonly referred to as the template function, which can be invoked with an object containing the values that are going to be interpolated in the template. The result of the invocation of the template function is a string value, which is the result of the interpolation of the provided values inside the template:

```
var templateFn = _.template('<h1><%= title %></h1>');
var resultHtml = templateFn({
  title: 'Underscore.js example'
});
```

As an example, the above code returns <h1>Underscore.js example</h1> and is equivalent to the following shorthand invocation:

```
var resultHtml = _.template('<h1><%= title %></h1>')({
  title: 'Underscore.js example'
});
```

For more information about the _.template method, you can read the documentation at: http://underscorejs.org/#template.

What makes `Underscore.js` templates very flexible is the `<% %>` notation, which allows us to perform any method invocation and is, for example, used as the recommended way to create loops in a template. On the other hand, overusing this feature may add too much logic to your templates, which is a known anti-pattern found in many other frameworks, violating the principle of **Separation of Concerns**.

Using Underscore.js templates in our applications

As an example of using `Underscore.js` for templating, we will now use it to refactor the HTML code generation which takes place in some modules of the dashboard example, as we saw in previous chapters. The modifications required to the existing implementation are limited to the `categories` and the `informationBox` modules, which manipulate the DOM tree of the page by adding new elements.

The first place that such a refactor can be applied is in the `init()` method of the `categories` module. We can modify the code that creates the available `<option>`s of the `<select>` category to look like this:

```
var optionTemplate = _.template(
  '<option value="<%= value %>"><%- title %></option>');
var optionsHtmlArray = [];
for (var i = 0; i < dashboard.categories.data.length; i++) {
    var categoryInfo = dashboard.categories.data[i];
    optionsHtmlArray.push(optionTemplate({
        value: i,
        title: categoryInfo.title
    }));
}
$categoriesSelector.append(optionsHtmlArray.join(''));
```

As you can see, we iterate over the categories of the dashboard in order to create and append the appropriate `<option>` elements to the `<select>` category element. In our template, we are using the `<%= %>` notation for the `value` attribute of the `<option>` since we know that it will hold an integer value that does not need escaping. On the other hand, we are using the `<%- %>` notation for the content part of each `<option>` in order to escape the title of each category for the case its value is not an HTML-safe string.

We are using the `_.template()` method outside the `for` loop in order to create a single compiled template function that will be reused on each iteration of the `for` loop. In this way, the browser not only executes the `_.template()` method just once, but also optimizes the generated template function and makes it run faster on each subsequent execution inside the `for` loop. Lastly, we are using the `join('')` method to combine all the HTML strings of the `optionsHtmlArray` variable and `append()` the result to the DOM with a single operation.

An alternative and possibly simpler way to achieve the same result is by combining the `<% %>` notation and the `_.each()` method that `Underscore.js` provides, enabling us to implement a loop inside the template itself. In this way, the template will be responsible for the iteration over the provided array of categories, moving the complexity from the implementation of the module into the template.

```
var templateSource = ''.concat(
    '<% _.each(categoryInfos, function(categoryInfo, i) { %>',
        '<option value="<%= i %>"><%- categoryInfo.title %></option>',
    '<% }); %>');
var optionsHtml = _.template(templateSource)({
    categoryInfos: dashboard.categories.data
});
$categoriesSelector.append(optionsHtml);
```

As you can see in the above code, our JavaScript implementation no longer contains a `for` loop, reducing its complexity and the required nesting. There is only a single call to the `_.template()` method, which nicely abstracts the implementation to an operation that generates the HTML and renders the `<option>` elements for all the categories. You can also see how nicely this technique fits in with the Composite logic that jQuery itself follows, in which the methods are designed to operate over collections of elements instead of single items.

Separating HTML templates from JavaScript code

Even after introducing all of the above improvements, it soon starts to become obvious that writing templates in between your application logic might not be the best approach to follow. As soon as your application becomes complex enough, or when you need to use templates that are more than a few lines long, the implementation starts to feel fragmented by the mix of the application's logic and the HTML templates.

A cleaner approach to this problem is to store your templates alongside the rest of the HTML code of your page. This is a good step towards better **Separation of Concerns** since it properly isolates the presentation from the application logic.

In order to include HTML templates as part of web pages in an inactive form, we need to use a host tag that will prevent them from being rendered, but also allow us to retrieve its content programmatically when needed. For this purpose, we can use `<script>` tags inside the `<head>` or the `<body>` of our page and specify any `type` other than the common `text/javascript` that we normally use for our JavaScript code. The operation principle behind this is that browsers do not try to parse, execute or render the content of `<script>` tags, in case their `type` attribute isn't recognized. After some experimentation, the community of `Underscore.js` users has largely adopted this practice and agreed to specify `text/template` as the preferred type for these `<script>` tags, in an attempt to make these implementations more uniform among developers.

Even though `Underscore.js` is neither opinionated nor contains any implementation specific to the way that the templates become available, using `text/template` `<script>` tags and/or AJAX requests have been valuable techniques that are widely used and are considered best practices.

As an example of a complex template that would be beneficial to move into a `<script>` tag, we will refactor to the `openNew()` method of the `informationBox` module. As you can see in the code below, the resulting `<script>` tag is cleanly formatted and we no longer need to use string concatenation for the definition of the multi-line template:

```html
<script id="box-template" type="text/template">
  <div class="boxsizer">
    <article class="box">
      <header class="boxHeader">
        <button class="boxCloseButton">&#10006;</button>
        <%- itemName %>
      </header>
      <div class="boxContent">Loading...</div>
    </article>
  </div>
</script>
```

A good practice when moving HTML templates out of our code is to write an abstracted mechanism to be responsible for retrieving them and providing the compiled template function. This approach not only decouples the rest of the implementation from the template retrieval mechanism but also makes it less repetitive and creates a centralized method designed to provide templates for the rest of the application. Moreover, as we can see below, this approach also allows us to optimize the way that templates are retrieved, propagating the benefits to all the places that they are used.

```javascript
var templateCache = {};

function getEmbeddedTemplate(templateName) {
    var compiledTemplate = templateCache[templateName];
    if (!compiledTemplate) {
        var template = $('#' + templateName).html();
        compiledTemplate = _.template(template);
        templateCache[templateName] = compiledTemplate;
    }
    return compiledTemplate;
}

dashboard.informationBox.openNew = function(itemName) {
    var boxCompiledTemplate = getEmbeddedTemplate('box-template');
    var boxHtml = boxCompiledTemplate({
        itemName: itemName
    });
    var $box = $(boxHtml).appendTo($boxContainer);

    /* ... */
};
```

As shown in the above implementation, the `openNew()` method of the `informationBox` module simply invokes the `getEmbeddedTemplate()` function by passing a unique identifier that is associated with the requested template and uses the returned template function to generate the new box's HTML and finally append it to the page. The most interesting part of the implementation is the `getEmbeddedTemplate()` method, which uses the `templateCache` variable as a dictionary to hold all the previously compiled template functions.

The first step is always to check whether the requested template identifier exists in our template cache. If not, then the DOM tree of the page is searched for the `<script>` tag with the related ID and its HTML content is used to create the template function, which is then stored in the cache and returned to the caller.

Keep in mind that it is a good practice to use a specific prefix or suffix for all the identifiers of your HTML templates in order to avoid conflicts with the IDs of other page elements. For this purpose, in the above example we used the `-template` as a suffix of the identifier of our box template.

Ideally, the implementation of the template provider method should be in a separate module that will be used by all the parts of an application but, since in our dashboard this is used in only one place, we met the needs of our demonstration by simply using a function.

Introducing Handlebars.js

Handlebars.js, or simply Handlebars, is a specialized client-side templating library that enables web developers to create semantic templates effectively. Using Handlebars for templating leads to the creation of logic-free templates which ensures that the view and the code are isolated, helping preserve the Separation of Concerns principle. It is largely compatible with Mustache templates, which are a templating language specification that have proven their effectiveness over time and have many implementations for all the major programming languages. Additionally, Handlebars provides a set of extensions on top of the Mustache template specification, such as helper methods and partials, as a means of extending the templating engine and creating more effective templates.

 You can see all the documentation for Handlebars at: `http://handlebarsjs.com/`. You can get more information about Mustache in JavaScript at: `https://github.com/janl/mustache.js/`.

The main template notation that Handlebars provides is the double curly braces syntax `{{ }}`. As Handlebars was designed to be used for HTML templates from the beginning, this notation also applies HTML escaping by default, lowering the chances that a non-escaped value could reach the template causing potential security problems. If a non-escaped interpolation is required for a specific part of a template, we can use the triple curly braces notation `{{{ }}}`.

Moreover, since Handlebars prevents us from invoking methods directly from within a template, it provides us with the ability to define and use helper methods and block expressions as a way to cover more complex use cases while also helping to maintain our templates as clean and readable as possible. The set of built-in helpers includes the `{{#if }}` and `{{#each }}` helpers which allow us to perform iterations over arrays and change the outcomes of a template based on conditions very easily.

The central method of the Handlebars library is the `Handlebars.compile()` method, which accepts a template string as a parameter and returns a function that can be used to generate string values that follow the form of the provided template. This function can then be invoked (as in `Underscore.js`) with an object as a parameter, the properties of which will be used as a context for the evaluation of all the Handlebars expressions (the curly braces notations) that were defined in the original template:

```
var templateFn = Handlebars.compile('<h1>!!!{{ title }}!!!</h1>');
var resultHtml = templateFn({
  title: '> Handlebars example <'
});
```

As an example, the above code returns `"<h1>!!!&gt; Handlebars example &lt;!!!</h1>"`, turning the interpolated title into a safe HTML string, but one which would otherwise render properly when attached to the DOM tree of a page. Of course, the same result can be achieved with the following shorthand invocation, if we don't need to keep a reference to the compiled template function for future use:

```
var resultHtml = Handlebars.compile('<h1>!!!{{ title }}!!!</h1>')({
  title: '> Handlebars example <'
});
```

Using Handlebars.js in our applications

As an example of using `Handlebars.js` for templating and in order to demonstrate its differences from `Underscore.js` templates, we will now use it to refactor our dashboard example, like we did in the previous section. Like before, the refactoring is limited to the `categories` and the `informationBox` modules, which manipulate the DOM tree of the page by adding new elements.

The refactored implementation of the `init()` method of the `categories` module should look like this:

```
var optionTemplate = Handlebars.compile(
  '<option value= "{{ value }}">{{ title }}</option>');
var optionsHtmlArray = [];
for (var i = 0; i < dashboard.categories.data.length; i++) {
    var categoryInfo = dashboard.categories.data[i];
    optionsHtmlArray .push(optionTemplate({
        value: i,
```

```
        title: categoryInfo.title
    }));
}
$categoriesSelector.append(optionsHtmlArray.join(''));
```

First of all, we have used the `Handlebars.compile()` method which generates and returns a template function based on the provided template string. The main difference with the `Underscore.js` implementation we saw in the previous section, is that we now use the double curly braces notation `{{ }}` to interpolate values in our template. Apart from the different appearance, `Handlebars.js` also does HTML string escaping by default in an attempt to eliminate HTML injection security holes by making escaping part of its primary use case.

As we did earlier in this chapter, we will create the template function outside the `for` loop and use it to generate the HTML for each `<option>` element. All the generated HTML strings are gathered in an array and are finally combined and attached to the DOM tree with a single operation, using the `$.append()` method.

The next incremental step to reduce the complexity of our implementation is to abstract the iterations away from our JavaScript code using the looping capabilities of the templating engine itself:

```
var templateSource = ''.concat(
    '{{#each categoryInfos}}',
        '<option value="{{@index}}">{{ title }}</option>',
    '{{/each}}');
var optionsHtml = Handlebars.compile(templateSource)({
    categoryInfos: dashboard.categories.data
});
$categoriesSelector.append(optionsHtml);
```

The `Handlebars.js` library allows us to achieve that by using the special `{{#each }}` notation. In between the `{{#each }}` and `{{/each}}`, the context of the template is changed to match each individual object of the iteration, allowing to directly access and interpolate the `{{ title }}` of each object in the `categoryInfos` array. Moreover, in order to access the loop counter, Handlebars provides us with the special `@index` variable as part of the context of the loop.

 For a full list of all the special notations that Handlebars provides, you can read the documentation at: `http://handlebarsjs.com/reference.html`

Separating HTML templates from JavaScript code

Like most templating engines, Handlebars also leads us to isolate our templates from the JavaScript implementation of our application and deliver them to the browser by including them in `<script>` tags, inside the HTML of our pages. Moreover, Handlebars is opinionated and prefers the special `text/x-handlebars-template` as the type attribute for all `<script>` tags that contain Handlebars templates. For example, here is how the template for the dashboard's boxes should be defined according to the library recommendations:

```html
<script id="box-template" type="text/x-handlebars-template">
  <div class="boxsizer">
    <article class="box">
      <header class="boxHeader">
        <button class="boxCloseButton">&#10006;</button>
        {{ itemName }}
      </header>
      <div class="boxContent">Loading...</div>
    </article>
  </div>
</script>
```

 Even though our implementation would still work if a different `type` was specified for the `<script>` tag, following the library's guidelines can obviously make implementations more uniform among developers.

As we did earlier in this chapter, we will follow the best practice of creating a separate function to be responsible for providing the templates wherever they are needed in the application:

```javascript
var templateCache = {};

function getEmbeddedTemplate(templateName) {
    var compiledTemplate = templateCache[templateName];
    if (!compiledTemplate) {
        var template = $('#' + templateName).html();
        compiledTemplate = Handlebars.compile(template);
        templateCache[templateName] = compiledTemplate;
    }
    return compiledTemplate;
}
```

```
dashboard.informationBox.openNew = function(itemName) {
    var boxCompiledTemplate = getEmbeddedTemplate('box-template');
    var boxHtml = boxCompiledTemplate({
        itemName: itemName
    });
    var $box = $(boxHtml).appendTo($boxContainer);

    /* ... */
};
```

As you can see, the implementation is mostly the same as the Undescore.js example that we saw earlier in this chapter. The only difference is that we are now using the Handlebars.compile() method to generate the compiled template functions from the retrieved templates.

Pre-compiling templates

An extra feature of the Handlebars library is the support for template pre-compilation. This allows us to pre-generate all the template functions with a simple terminal command and then have our server deliver to them to the browser, instead of the actual templates. In this way, the browser will be able to use the pre-compiled templates directly, removing the need for the compilation of each individual template and making the execution of the library and our application faster.

In order to pre-compile our templates, we first need to place them in separate files. The Handlebars documentation suggests using the .handlebars extension for our files but we can still use the .html extension if it is preferred. After installing the compilation tool on our development machine (with npm install handlebars -g), we can issue the following command in our terminal to compile a template:

handlebars box-template.handlebars -f box-template.js

This will generate the box-template.js file that is actually a mini-module definition that adds the template to Handlebars.templates. The generated file can then be combined and minified like regular JavaScript files and, when loaded by a browser, the template function will become available through the Handlebars.templates['box-template'] property.

 Keep in mind that if the .html extension is being used for the templates, then the pre-compiled template function will be available through the Handlebars.templates['box-template.html'] property.

As you can see, using a template provider function assists with the migration of an existing application to pre-compiled templates since it allows us to encapsulate the way that the templates are retrieved. Moving to pre-compiled templates only requires changing the `getEmbeddedTemplate()` to something like this:

```
function getEmbeddedTemplate(templateName) {
    return Handlebars.templates[templateName];
}
```

 For more information about template pre-compilation in Handlebars, read the documentation at: `http://handlebarsjs.com/precompilation.html`.

Retrieving HTML templates asynchronously

The final step to mastering client-side templating is a development practice that allows us to load templates dynamically and use them in a web page that has already been loaded. This approach can lead to more scalable implementations than the approach of embedding all the available templates as `<script>` tags inside the HTML source of each page.

The key element of this technique is to load each template only when it is required for the presentation of a web page, commonly after a user action. The main benefits of this approach are that:

- The initial page load time is reduced since the HTML of the page is smaller. The gains from the reduction of the page size become even greater if our application has a lot of templates that are used only under certain circumstances, for example, after specific user interactions.

- The user only downloads a template if it is actually going to be used. In this way, the size of the total downloaded resources for each page load can be reduced.

- Subsequent requests for an already loaded template will not lead to an extra download, since the browser's HTTP caching mechanism will return the cached resource. Additionally, since the browser cache is used for all HTTP requests regardless of the page from which they originate, users only have to download the required template once while using our web application.

Because of its benefits to user experience and its scalability, this technique is widely used by the most popular webmail and social networking web sites, where various HTML templates and JavaScript modules are loaded dynamically, based on user actions.

 For more information on how jQuery can be used to load JavaScript modules on a page dynamically, read the documentation for the `$.getScript()` method at: `https://api.jquery.com/jQuery.getScript/`.

Adopting it in an existing implementation

To illustrate this technique, we will change the Underscore.js and Handlebars.js implementations of the `informationBox` module so that it fetches the box template for our dashboard using an AJAX request.

Let's proceed by analyzing the necessary changes for our Underscore.js implementation:

```
var templateCache = {};

function getAjaxTemplate(templateName) {
    var compiledTemplate = templateCache[templateName];
    if (compiledTemplate) {
        return $.Deferred().resolve(compiledTemplate);
    }
    return $.ajax({
        mimeType: 'text/html',
        url: templateName + '.html'
    }).then(function(template) {
        templateCache[templateName] = _.template(template);
        return templateCache[templateName];
    });
}
```

As you can see in the above code, we have implemented the `getAjaxTemplate()` function as a way of decoupling the mechanism that is responsible for fetching the template from the implementation that uses it. This implementation has a lot in common with the `getEmbeddedTemplate()` function that we used earlier, the main difference being that the `getAjaxTemplate()` function is asynchronous and, as a result, returns a **Promise**.

The `getAjaxTemplate()` function firstly checks whether or not the requested template already exists in its cache, as an extra attempt to reduce HTTP requests to the server. If the template is found in the cache, then it is returned as part of a Resolved Promise, otherwise we initiate an AJAX request using the `$.ajax()` method to retrieve it from the server. Like before, we need to have a convention regarding the naming of the template HTML files and the path used to store them in the server. In our example, we are looking in the same directory as the web page itself and just appending the `.html` file extension. An extra concern in some cases, depending on the web server used, is the definition of the `mimeType` of the resource as `text/html`.

When the AJAX request completes, the `then()` method is executed with the content of the template as a string parameter, which is used to generate the compiled template function. Our implementation finally returns the compiled template function as the result of the chained Promise, right after adding it to its cache. Since the `getAjaxTemplate()` function is asynchronous, we also had to change the implementation of the `openNew()` method and move all the code using the returned template function inside a `then()` callback. Apart from this, the implementation has remained the same and uses the template function in exactly the same way as before.

```
dashboard.informationBox.openNew = function(itemName) {
    var templatePromise = getAjaxTemplate('box-template');
    templatePromise.then(function(boxCompiledTemplate) {
        var boxHtml = boxCompiledTemplate({
            itemName: itemName
        });
        var $box = $(boxHtml).appendTo($boxContainer); box);
        /* ... */
    });
};
```

When re-implementing the `getAjaxTemplate()` function to use `Handlebars.js`, the resulting code is mostly the same as before. The only difference is in the invocation of the `Handlebars.compile()` method instead of the `Undescore.js` equivalent. This is an added benefit as many client-side templating engines influenced each other and have converged into a very similar API regarding the way that their template functions are used, largely because of the positive user feedback on the existing implementations.

```
function getAjaxTemplate(templateName) {
    /* …same as before... */
    return $.ajax({ /* …same as before... */
    }).then(function(template) {
```

```
templateCache[templateName] =
    Handlebars.compile(template);
return templateCache[templateName];
    });
}
```

Keep in mind that the `$.ajax()` method might not work in some browsers when the page is loaded through the filesystem, but works as intended when served using a web server like Apache, IIS, or nginx.

Moderation is best in all things

Even though this technique reduces the overall download footprint of each web page, it also inevitably increases the number of HTTP requests made. Moreover, the practice of loading every template lazily can sometimes increase the time that the user will have to wait if the templates are required for the initial rendering of the page.

Balancing the way that we load our templates between lazy loading and embedding them in `<script>` tags usually brings the best of both worlds. This hybrid approach is considered a best practice by the industry since it allows us to micromanage and fine tune each implementation based on its needs. According to this practice, the templates that are required for the presentation of the main content of a page are embedded in its HTML, while the rest of them are delivered lazily when needed, taking advantage of browser caching.

The implementation of such a template provider function is left as an exercise for the reader. As a hint, such methods have to be asynchronous since, when the requested template is not found embedded in the `<script>` tag of the page, it will have to proceed and make an AJAX request to retrieve it from the server.

Keep in mind that it is generally preferable to generate the complete initial HTML content of the page on the server side instead of using client-side templating. This not only leads to a smaller loading time of the initial page content but it also prevents situations in which the user is presented with an empty page when JavaScript is unavailable or an error has occurred.

Summary

In this chapter, we learned how to use two of the most common client-side templating libraries: Underscore.js and Handlebars.js. We also learned how they allow us to create complex HTML templates faster while making our implementations easier to read and understand. We then went on to analyze their conventions and evaluate their features and learned by example how they can be effectively and efficiently used in our implementations.

After completing this chapter, we are now able to generate complex HTML structures in a browser efficiently by using readable templates and utilizing the unique characteristics of the templating libraries.

In the next chapter, we will learn how to create jQuery Plugins as a way to abstract parts of our applications into reusable and extensible implementations. We will introduce the most widely used patterns for developing jQuery Plugins and analyze the implementation problems that each of them helps to solve.

10
Plugin and Widget Development Patterns

This chapter focuses on the design patterns and best practices used when implementing jQuery Plugins. We will learn here how to abstract parts of an application into separate jQuery Plugins, promoting the **Separation of Concerns** principle and code reusability.

We will firstly analyze the simplest ways that a jQuery Plugin can be implemented, learn the various conventions of jQuery Plugin development and the basic characteristics that every plugin should satisfy in order to follow jQuery principles. We will then proceed with an introduction to the most widely used design patterns and analyze the characteristics and benefits of each of them. By the end of this chapter, we will be able to implement extensible jQuery Plugins using the development pattern that best suits each use case.

In this chapter we will:

- Introduce the jQuery Plugin API and its conventions
- Analyze the characteristics that make an excellent plugin
- Learn how to create a plugin by extending the $.fn object
- Learn how to implement generic plugins that are extensible in order to make them reusable in more use cases
- Learn how to provide options and methods to your plugins
- Introduce the most common design patterns for jQuery plugin development and analyze the common implementation problems that each of them helps to solve

Introducing jQuery Plugins

The key concept of jQuery plugins lies in extending the jQuery API by making their functionality accessible as a method on jQuery **Composite Collection** Objects. A jQuery plugin is simply a function that is defined as a new method on the $.fn object, which is the **Prototype Object** that every jQuery Collection Object inherits from.

```
$.fn.simplePlugin101 = function(arg1, arg2/*, ...*/) {
    // Plugin's implementation...
};
```

By defining a method on the $.fn object, we are actually extending the core jQuery API itself, since this makes the method available on all created jQuery Collection Objects from that point onwards. As a result, after a plugin has been loaded in a web page, its functionality is available as a method on every object returned by the $() function:

```
$('h1').simplePlugin101('test', 1);
```

The main convention of the jQuery plugin API is that the jQuery Collection Object that the plugin was invoked on is made available to the plugin's method as its execution context. In other words, we can use the this identifier in the plugin method, as shown below:

```
$.fn.simplePlugin101 = function() {
    this.slideToggle();
    // "this" is a jQuery object where all
    // jQuery methods are available
};
```

Following jQuery principles

One of the goals when creating a plugin is to make it feel like a part of jQuery itself. After reading the previous chapters, you should be familiar with some of the principles that all jQuery methods follow and the characteristics that make its approach special. Implementing a plugin that follows these principles makes users feel more comfortable with its API, be more productive, and make fewer implementation errors, which leads to an increase in the plugin's popularity and adoption.

Two of the most important characteristics that a great jQuery plugin should have are as follows:

- It should apply on all the elements of the jQuery Collection Object it is invoked on whenever applicable
- It should allow further chaining of other jQuery methods

Let's now move on and analyze each of these principles.

Working on Composite Collection Objects

One of the most important features of jQuery methods is that they are applied on every item of the Composite Collection Object that they are invoked on. As an example, the `$.fn.addClass()` method adds one or more CSS classes to every item of the collection after individually checking whether each class has already been defined on each individual element.

As a result, our jQuery plugins should also follow this principle by operating on every element of a collection, when such a thing seems logical. If you are using only jQuery methods in your plugin's implementation, most of the time, you get this for free. On the other hand, an important consideration to bear in mind is that not all jQuery methods operate on every element of a collection object. Methods like `$.fn.html()`, `$.fn.css()` and `$.fn.data()` apply on all the items of the collection when used as setter methods, but operate only on the first element when used as getters.

Let's see an example implementation of a plugin that uses `$.fn.animate()` to create a shake effect on all items of a jQuery object:

```
$.fn.vibrate = function() {
  this.each(function(i, element) {
    // specifically handle every element
    var $element = $(element);
    if ($element.css('position') === 'static') {
      $element.css({ position: 'relative' });
    }
  });

  this.animate({ left: '+=3' }, 30)
    .animate({ left: '-=6' }, 60)
    .animate({ left: '+=6' }, 60)
    .animate({ left: '-=3' }, 30);

  return this; // allow further chaining
};
```

Invoking this plugin with `$('button').vibrate();` applies the shaking animation on every matched element of the page. To achieve that, the plugin changes the `left` CSS property of all matched elements using the `$.fn.animate()` method, which conveniently operates on every element. On the other hand, since the `$.fn.css()` method applies only on the first element of the collection when used as a getter, we had to iterate over all the elements using the `$.fn.each()` method and ensure that each of them was not statically positioned, in which case the `left` CSS property would not affect its appearance.

Obviously, using only jQuery methods is not always sufficient for the implementation of a plugin. In most cases, a new plugin will have to use at least one non-jQuery API for its implementation, requiring us to iterate over the items of the collection and apply the logic of the plugin to each of them individually. The same approach should be used when each element of the collection has to be handled slightly differently based on its state.

As a result, it is quite common for plugins to wrap almost all of their implementations inside a `$.fn.each()` invocation. By recognizing the common needs that are covered by explicit iteration, the jQuery team and most jQuery plugin boilerplates now make it part of their standard practice.

Allowing further chaining

In general, when your plugin's code does not need to return anything, all that you have to do to enable further chaining is to add a `return this;` statement to its last line, as we saw in the previous example. Make sure that all the code paths return a reference of the invocation context (`this`) or another relevant jQuery collection object, in the same way that `$.fn.parent()` and `$.fn.find()` do. Alternatively, when all your code is wrapped inside another jQuery method, such as `$.fn.each()`, it is common practice to simply return the result of that invocation, as demonstrated below:

```
$.fn.myLogPlugin = function() {
    return this.each(function(i, element) {
        console.log($(element).text());
    });
};
```

Keep in mind that, if your code manipulates the collection object that it was invoked on, instead of returning the `this` reference, you might need to return the new collection that was the result of your plugin's manipulations.

You should avoid basing your plugin's implementation on a return value in order to allow further chaining. Instead of doing that, it is preferable to initialize the plugin on its first invocation and then provide some overloaded ways to invoke it, as a way of returning values.

Working with $.noConflict()

The first step to improve a plugin's implementation is to make it work in environments that do not have access to the $ identifier. An example of this is when a web page uses the `jQuery.noConflict()` method, which prevents jQuery from assigning itself to the $ global identifier (or `window.$`) and keeps it available only on the `jQuery` namespace (`window.jQuery`).

The `jQuery.noConflict()` method allows us to prevent jQuery from conflicting with other libraries and implementations that also happen to use the $ variable. For more information, you can visit the jQuery documentation page at: `http://api.jquery.com/jQuery.noConflict/`

In such cases, the plugin definition would throw an **$ is not defined** error or even worse; it might try to use the $ variable that the developer has reserved to use in an implementation, leading to errors that are hard to debug.

Fortunately, the changes required to fix this problem are easy to implement and do not affect the functionality of the plugin. All that we have to do is rename all of the occurrences of the $ identifier in our plugin with `jQuery`, as shown below:

```
jQuery.fn.simplePlugin101 = function(arg1, arg2/*, ...*/) {
    var $buttons = jQuery('button');
    // ...
};
```

Wrapping with an IIFE

The next best practice to follow is to wrap the definition and implementation of our plugin with an IIFE. This not only makes our plugin look like the **Module Pattern** but also makes our implementation more robust by adding several other benefits to it.

First of all, the IIFE pattern allows us to create and use private variables and functions in the context of the plugin's definition. These variables are shared across all the instances of the plugin in a similar way to how static variables work in other programming languages, enabling us to use them as synchronization points between the plugin instances:

```
(function($) {
    var callCounter = 0;

    function utilityLogMethod(message) {
        if (window.console && console.log) {
            console.log(message);
        }
    }

    $.fn.simplePlugin101 = function(arg1, arg2/*, ...*/) {
        callCounter++;
        utilityLogMethod(callCounter);
        return this;
    };
})(jQuery);
```

Otherwise, we would have to use something like `$._simplePlugin101._callCounter` or `$._simplePlugin101._utilityLogMethod()` to emulate privacy, which is just a naming convention and does not provide any actual privacy.

The second benefit, as demonstrated in the above example, is that it allows us to use the `$` identifier again to access jQuery with no concerns about conflicts. In order to achieve this, we are passing the jQuery namespace variable as an invocation parameter to our IIFE and use the `$` identifier to name the respective parameter. In this way, we effectively alias the jQuery namespace to `$` in the context created by the IIFE, enabling us to use the minimal `$` identifier in our implementation to keep our code slim and readable, even if `jQuery.noConflict()` is used.

Additionally, adding the `use strict;` statement on the top of our IIFE helps us to eliminate any leaking of variables into the global namespace. For example, the following code would throw a **ReferenceError: assignment to undeclared variable x** error during the invocation of the plugin's method, enabling us to catch those errors during the development phase of the plugin helping produce a more robust final implementation:

```
(function($) {
    'use strict';

    $.fn.leakingPlugin = function() {
```

```
    x = 0;
    // there is no "var x" declaration,
    // so an error is thrown when executed
  };
})(jQuery);

$('div').leakingPlugin();
```

 For more information about JavaScript's strict execution mode, you can visit: `https://developer.mozilla.org/en-US/docs/Web/JavaScript/Reference/Strict_mode`

Finally, this pattern, as with all the namespace aliasing practices that use IIFEs, can also help increase the gains when minifying your plugin's source code, when compared to an implementation that references the jQuery namespace variable directly. In an attempt to maximize the benefits of this technique, it's also common to alias all the global namespace variables that our plugin accesses, as demonstrated below:

```
(function ( $, window, document, undefined ) {
    // Plugin's implementation...
})( jQuery, window, document );
```

Creating reusable plugins

After analyzing the most important aspects of the development of jQuery plugins, we are now ready to analyze an implementation that is used for something more than a simple demonstration. In order to create a really useful and reusable plugin, it must be designed such that its operations are not restricted by the demands of its original use case.

The most popular plugins, like the most useful jQuery methods, are those that provide a high degree of configuration of their functionality. Creating a plugin that is configurable adds a degree of flexibility to its implementation, which enables us to match the needs of several other use cases that are governed by the same operation principles.

As we said earlier, a jQuery plugin is just a function attached to the $.fn object and, as a result, we can make its implementation more abstract and generic in the same way as with plain functions of our modules. As in simple functions, the easiest way to differentiate the operation of a jQuery plugin is by using invocation parameters. A plugin that exposes a lot of configuration parameters has great potential of being able to be match the requirements of several different use cases.

Accepting configuration parameters

In contrast to how we implement functions that usually accept up to five arguments and still have a manageable and relatively clean API, this practice does not work so well with jQuery plugins. In order to expose a clear API and maintain a high level of usability, regardless of the various configuration options that are exposed, most jQuery plugins provide a minimal API that accepts up to three invocation arguments. This is achieved by using dedicated setting objects with a specific format, as a way of encapsulating multiple options and passing them as a single argument. Another approach is to expose an API with two parameters, where the first one is a regular value that defines the operation of the plugin and the second one is used to wrap the less important configuration options.

A great example of both of these practices is the `$.ajax(settings)` method, which is invoked with a single settings object as a parameter to define how it should operate, but also exposes another overloaded way to be invoked with two arguments. The two argument overload is invoked with `$.ajax(url, settings)`, where the first is the target URL for the HTTP request and the second is an object with the rest configuration options. What applies to both of them is that the method itself contains a set of sensible defaults that are used instead of any configuration parameter that the user has not defined. Moreover, the second overload also defines the second parameter as optional and, if that was not provided during its invocation, it bases its operation on the default settings.

Adopting the settings object practice in our plugins not only brings all the aforementioned benefits, but also allows us to extend the implementation in a more scalable way, since the addition of an extra configuration parameter has little effect on the rest of its API. As an example of this, we will reimplement the `$.fn.vibrate` plugin that we saw earlier in this chapter in a more generic way, so that a setting object with default values is used for its configuration:

```
(function($) {

  $.fn.vibrate = function(options) {
    var opts = $.extend({}, $.fn.vibrate.defaultOptions, options);

    this.each(function(i, element) {
      var $element = $(element);
      if ($element.css('position') === 'static') {
        $element.css({ position: 'relative' });
      }
    });

    for (var i = 0, len = opts.loops * 4; i < len; i++) {
```

```
    var animationProperties = {};
    var movement = (i % 2) ? '+=': '-=';

    movement += (i === 0 || i === len - 1) ?
      opts.amplitude / 2:
      opts.amplitude;

    var t = (i === 0 || i === len - 1) ?
      opts.period / 4:
      opts.period / 2;

    animationProperties[opts.direction] = movement;
    this.animate(animationProperties, t);
  }

  return this;
};

$.fn.vibrate.defaultOptions = {
  loops: 2,
  amplitude: 8,
  period: 100,
  direction: 'left'
};
})(jQuery);
```

In contrast to the original fixed implementation, this one accepts a single object as an invocation parameter which wraps four different options that can be used to diversify the operation of the plugin. The options object allows us to diversify the operation of the plugin by exposing four customization points:

- The number of loops that the shake effect should run
- The amplitude of the animation, as a means of controlling how much an element should move away from its original position
- The period of each loop, as a means of controlling how fast the movement will be
- The direction of the animation, which is horizontal when left is used or vertical when top is used

By following a widely accepted best practice, we have defined all the default values for the configuration options as a separate object. This pattern not only allows us to gather all the related values under a single object, but also enables us to use the `$.extend()` method as an effective way of composing all the defined options with the default values of the undefined ones. We can thus avoid checking explicitly for the existence of each individual property, reducing the complexity and the size of our code.

In brief, the `$.extend()` method returns the object passed as its first argument after merging the properties of the subsequent objects together into the first object. As a result, the returned object will contain all the default values except those that were defined in the options object that was passed as an invocation parameter.

> For more information about the `$.extend()` helper method, you can visit the documentation page at: `http://api.jquery.com/jQuery.extend/`

Moreover, instead of using a simple variable, we are exposing the default options object as a property of the plugin's function, enabling users to change them to better suit their needs. As an example, consider a case in which a smooth animation is required for the needs of a specific application. By setting `$.fn.vibrate.defaultOptions.period = 250`, the developer would completely remove the need to specify the `period` option in every invocation of the plugin, which would lead to an implementation with less repetitive code.

> The jQuery library itself adopts this practice for defining the default configuration parameters of the `$.ajax()` method. Because of the increased complexity of this method, jQuery provides us with the `jQuery.ajaxSetup()` method as a way of setting up the default parameters for every AJAX request.

Finally, in order to create a generic variant of the original implementation and utilize the aforementioned configuration options, we replaced the four fixed invocations of the `$.fn.animate()` method of the original implementation with a `for` loop that utilized the `loops` option. Inside the `for` loop itself, we construct the parameters for each call of the `$.fn.animate()` method and briefly alternate the direction of the animated movement on each subsequent execution of the loop, and also ensure that the first and last movements have half of the time duration and half of the shift of all of the other steps.

The final implementation can be configured to produce different animations, based on the needs of each specific use case, ranging from short horizontal animations that are ideal for notifying a user about an invalid action, to vertical long animations that look like a levitation effect. The plugin can be invoked with any combination of the aforementioned options, use the default values for missing options and even operate with no invocation argument, as shown below:

```
// do the default intense animation on a button
// that appears disabled, to designate an invalid action
$('button.disabled').on('click', function() {
  $(this).vibrate();
});

// do a smother shake animation to catch the user's
// attention on an important part of the page
$('.save-button').vibrate({loops: 3, period: 250});

// start a long running levitation effect on the header of the page
$('h1').vibrate({direction: 'top', loops: 1000, period: 5000});
```

Writing stateful jQuery plugins

The plugin implementations that we have looked at so far were stateless since, after completing their execution, they revert their manipulations on the DOM's state and don't leave allocated objects in the browser's memory. As a result, subsequent invocations of stateless plugins always produce the same results.

As you can probably guess, such plugins have limited applications since they can't be used to create a series of complex interactions with the user of the web page. In order to orchestrate complex user interactions, a plugin needs to preserve an internal state with the actions taken up to that point in order to change its operation mode appropriately and handle subsequent interactions. Comparing the characteristic of stateful and stateless plugins could be defined as the equivalent to comparing plain (static) functions with methods that are part of an object and can operate on its state.

Another popular category of plugins, in which having an internal state is essential, is the family of plugins that manipulate the DOM tree. These plugins usually create complex element structures such as a rich text editors, date pickers and calendars, commonly by building on a user-defined empty `<div>` element.

Implementing a stateful jQuery Plugin

As an example of the patterns used for the implementation of plugins of this family, we will write a generic **Element Mutation Observer** plugin. This plugin will provide us with a convenient way of adding event listeners for changes to the DOM tree that originate from any of the elements that this plugin was invoked on. As a way of achieving that, the following implementation uses the **MutationObserver** API, which, at the time of writing, is implemented by all modern browsers and is available to more than 86% of web users.

 For more information on the Mutation Observer, you can visit: https://developer.mozilla.org/en-US/docs/Web/API/ MutationObserver

Let's now proceed with the implementation and analyze the practices that were used:

```
(function($) {
  $.fn.mutationObserver = function(action) {
    return this.each(function(i, element) {
      var $element = $(element);
      var instance = $element.data('plugin_mutationObserver');

      if (!instance) {
        var observer = new MutationObserver(function(mutations) {
          mutations.forEach(function(mutation) {
            instance.callbacks.forEach(function(callbackFn) {
              callbackFn(mutation);
            });
          });
        });

        observer.observe(element, {
          attributes: true,
          childList: true,
          characterData: true
        });

        instance = {
          observer: observer,
          callbacks: []
        };
        $element.data('plugin_mutationObserver', instance);
      }
```

```
    if (typeof action === 'function') {
      instance.callbacks.push(action);
    }
  });

  };
}) (jQuery);
```

Firstly, we define our plugin inside an IIFE, as recommended earlier in this chapter. Right after the declaration of the plugin on the $.fn object, we use the $.fn.each() method as a direct approach to ensure that the functionality of our plugin is applied to every item of the jQuery Collection Object that it was invoked on.

Two of the main issues that stateful plugin implementations have is the lack of a mechanism to preserve the internal state of each instantiation of the plugin and a way of avoiding being initialized many times on the same page element. In order to solve both of these problems, we need to use something like a hash table in which the key is the element itself and the value is an object with the state of the plugin's instance.

Fortunately, this is more or less how the $.fn.data() method works by associating DOM elements and JavaScript object values using specific string keys. By using the $.fn.data() method and the plugin's name as an association key, we are able to store and retrieve the state object of our plugin very easily.

Using the $.fn.data() method for this use case is considered a best practice and is used by most stateful plugin implementations and boilerplates since it is a robust part of jQuery that enables us to reduce the size of our plugin's implementation.

If an existing state object is not found then we can assume that the plugin is not yet initialized on that specific element and start its initialization right away. The state object of this plugin will contain the instance of the active MutationObserver responsible for tracking the changes that happen on the observed DOM element, and an array with all the callbacks that have subscribed to it to get notifications about changes.

After creating a new MutationObserver instance, we configure it to look for three specific types of DOM changes and instruct it to invoke all the callbacks of the plugin's state object whenever such DOM changes occur. Finally, we create the state object itself to hold the observer and the associated callbacks and use the $.fn.data() method as a setter and associate it with the page element.

After ensuring that the plugin is instantiated and initialized on the provided element, we check whether the plugin is invoked with a function as a parameter and, if so, we add it to the list of the plugin's callbacks.

 Keep in mind that using a single MutationObserver instance per element and having it notify about DOM changes by iterating over an array of callbacks greatly reduces the memory requirements of the implementation, just like when we are using a single delegate observer.

An example of using our newly implemented plugin to observe for changes of a specific DOM element would look like this:

```
$('.container').mutationObserver(function(mutation) {
  console.log('Something changed on the DOM tree!');
});
```

Destroying a plugin instance

An extra consideration that a stateful plugin has to take into account is offering the developer a way to reverse the changes that it introduced to the state of the page. The most common and simple API for achieving this is to invoke the plugin with the `destroy` literal as its first parameter. Let's proceed with the required implementation changes:

```
(function($) {
  $.fn.mutationObserver = function(action) {
    return this.each(function(i, element) {
      var $element = $(element);
      var instance = $element.data('plugin_mutationObserver');

      if (action === 'destroy' && instance) {
        instance.observer.disconnect();
        instance.observer = null;
        $element.removeData('plugin_mutationObserver');
        return;
      }

      if (!instance) {
        /* ... */
      }
    });

  };
})(jQuery);
```

In order to adapt our implementation to the above requirement, all we had to do was to check whether the plugin was invoked with the `destroy` string value as its first parameter, right after retrieving the plugin's state object. If we find that the plugin has already been instantiated on the specified element and that the `destroy` string value has been used, we can proceed to stop the Mutation Observer itself and clear the association that `$.fn.data()` created by using the `$.fn.removeData()` method. Finally, at the end of the `if` statement we added a `return` statement since, after completing the destruction of the plugin instance, we no longer need to execute any other code. An example of destroying a plugin instance with this implementation would look like this:

```
$('.container').mutationObserver('destroy');
```

Implementing getter and setter methods

By using the same technique that we demonstrated earlier for the implementation of the `destroy` method of our plugin, we can provide several other overloaded ways to invoke our plugin that work like normal methods. This pattern is not only used by plain jQuery plugins, but is also adopted by more complex plugin architectures, as with jQuery-UI.

On the other hand, we might end up with a plugin implementation that results in a large number of invocation overloads, which is something that would make it difficult to use and document. A way to work around this is to combine the getter and setter methods of your API into multi-purpose methods. This not only reduces the API surface of your plugin so that a developer has to remember fewer method names but it also increases the productivity since the same pattern is used in many jQuery methods like `$.fn.html()`, `$.fn.css()`, `$.fn.prop()`, `$.fn.val()`, and `$.fn.data()`.

As a demonstration of this, let's see how we can add a new method to our MutationObserver plugin that works both as a getter and a setter for the registered callbacks:

```
(function($) {
  $.fn.mutationObserver = function(action, callbackFn) {
    var result = this;

    this.each(function(i, element) {
      var $element = $(element);
      var instance = $element.data('plugin_mutationObserver');
      /* ... */
```

```
      if (typeof action === 'function') {
        instance.callbacks.push(action);
      } else if (action === 'callbacks') {
        if (callbackFn && callbackFn.length >= 0) {
          // used as a setter
          instance.callbacks = callbackFn;
        } else {
          // used as a getter for the first element
          result = instance.callbacks;
          return false;// break the $.fn.each() iteration
        }
      }
    });

    return result;
  };
})(jQuery);
```

As shown in the above code, we have created an overloaded invocation method which uses the `callbacks` string value as the first argument of the plugin invocation. This getter and setter method allows us to retrieve or overwrite all of the callbacks that are registered on the MutationObserver and works in addition to the pre-existing methods for invoking the plugin, by using a function parameter and the `destroy` method.

The getter and setter implementation is based on the assumption that, when trying to use the `callbacks` method as a getter, you don't need to pass any extra parameters and, when trying to use it as a setter, you will pass an extra array as an invocation parameter. In order to support the getter variant, which prevents further chaining and only operates on the first element of the composite collection, we had to declare and use the `result` variable which is initialized to the value of the `this` identifier. If the `callbacks` getter is used, we assign the `callbacks` of the first element of the collection to the `result` variable and break out of the `$.fn.each()` iteration by returning `false` to finish the execution of the plugin's method.

Here is an example use case for our newly implemented getter and setter method:

```
// retrieve the callbacks
var oldCallbacks = $('.container').mutationObserver('callbacks');
// clear them
$('.container').mutationObserver('callbacks', []);
// add a new one
$('.container').mutationObserver(function() {
  console.log('Printed only once');
  // restore the old callbacks
  $('.container').mutationObserver('callbacks', oldCallbacks);
});
```

Keep in mind that invocation overloads that prevent further chaining by returning non-jQuery object results should be well documented since this technique conflicts with the chaining principle that everyone expects to work.

Using our plugin in our Dashboard application

After completing our `mutationObserver` plugin, lets now see how we can use it for the implementation of the `counter` sub-module that we used in our Dashboard's implementation in previous chapters:

```javascript
(function() {
    'use strict';
    dashboard.counter = dashboard.counter || {};

    var $counter;

    dashboard.counter.init = function() {
        $counter = $('#dashboardItemCounter');
        var $boxContainer = dashboard.$container
          .find('.boxContainer');

        $boxContainer.mutationObserver(function(mutation) {
            dashboard.counter.setValue(
                $boxContainer.children().length);
        });
    };

    dashboard.counter.setValue = function (value) {
        $counter.text(value);
    };
})();
```

As you can see in the above implementation, our plugin abstracts nicely and replaces the old implementation by providing a generic, flexible and reusable API. Instead of listening for click events on the different buttons of the page, the implementation is now using the `mutationObserver` plugin and observes the `boxContainer` element for the additions or removals of child elements. Moreover, this implementation change does not affect the functionality of the `counter` module which appears to work in the same way since all the changes are encapsulated in the module.

Using the jQuery Plugin Boilerplate

The jQuery Boilerplate project, which is available at `https://github.com/jquery-boilerplate/jquery-patterns`, offers several templates that can be used as starting points for the implementation of robust and extensible plugins. These templates incorporate a lot of best practices and design patterns such as those analyzed earlier in this chapter. Each of the templates packs a number of best practices that work well together, in an attempt to provide good starting points that better match the various use cases.

Perhaps the most widely used template is `jquery.basic.plugin-boilerplate` from Adam Sontag and Addy Osmani, which even though it is characterized as a generic template for beginners and above, successfully covers most aspects of jQuery plugin development. What makes this template unique is the Object-Oriented approach that it follows which is presented in such a way that it helps you write better structured code, without making it harder to introduce customizations on the implementation. Let's proceed and analyze its source code:

```
/*!
 * jQuery lightweight plugin boilerplate
 * Original author: @ajpiano
 * Further changes, comments: @addyosmani
 * Licensed under the MIT license
 */
;(function ( $, window, document, undefined ) {
  var pluginName = "defaultPluginName",
    defaults = {
      propertyName: "value"
    };
  function Plugin( element, options ) {
    this.element = element;
    this.options = $.extend( {}, defaults, options) ;
    this._defaults = defaults;
    this._name = pluginName;
    this.init();
  }
  Plugin.prototype = {
    init: function() { /* Place initialization logic here  */ },
    yourOtherFunction: function(options) { /* some logic */ }
  };
  // A really lightweight plugin wrapper around the constructor,
  // preventing against multiple instantiations
  $.fn[pluginName] = function ( options ) {
    return this.each(function () {
```

```
      if (!$.data(this, "plugin_" + pluginName)) {
        $.data(this, "plugin_" + pluginName,
        new Plugin( this, options ) );
      }
    });
  };


})( jQuery, window, document );
```

The semi-colon right before the IIFE is there to avoid errors in case of unfortunate script concatenation (and possibly minification) with a file that might be missing an ending semi-colon. Right below, the boilerplate uses the `pluginName` variable as a DRY way of naming our plugin and using its name for any other case. As an added benefit, all that we have to do if we need to rename our plugin is change the value of this variable and rename the `.js` file of our plugin accordingly.

Following the best practices that we saw earlier, a variable is used to hold the default options of the plugin and, as we can see a few lines later, it is merged with the user-provided options using the `$.extend()` method. Keep in mind that, if we want to expose the default options, all that we have to do is define it as part of the plugin's namespace: `$.fn[pluginName].defaultOptions = defaults;`

The actual plugin definition can be found near the end of this boilerplate code. Following the already discussed best practices, it iterates over the items of the collection using `$.fn.each()` and returns its result, which is equivalent to returning `this`. It then ensures that a plugin state instance exists for each item of the collection by using the `$.data()` method and the prefixed plugin name as an association key.

The `Plugin` constructor function is used for the creation of the plugin's state object which, after storing the DOM element and the final plugin options as properties of the object, invokes the `init()` method of its prototype. The `init()` method is the suggested place to define our initialization code, for example, it could instantiate a new MutationObserver as we did earlier in this chapter.

Adding methods to your plugin

By default, every method that is defined as part of the prototype is only available for internal use. On the other hand, we can easily extend the above implementation to make a method available to all our users, as shown below:

```
$.fn[pluginName] = function ( options, extraParam ) {
  return this.each(function () {
    var instance = $.data(this, "plugin_" + pluginName);
    if (!instance) {
```

```
      instance = new Plugin( this, options );
      $.data(this, "plugin_" + pluginName, instance);
    } else if (options === 'yourOtherFunction') {
      instance.yourOtherFunction(this, extraParam);
    }
  });
};
```

One guideline to follow when working with this boilerplate is to extend your plugin by adding extra methods to the `Plugin`'s prototype. Additionally, try to keep any modifications to the plugin's definition as small as possible, ideally single line method invocations.

In order to make the implementation more scalable, with regards to how the plugin methods are invoked and if we want to add an abstract approach for methods that are intended for internal or private use by the plugin, we can introduce the following changes:

```
$.fn[pluginName] = function ( options ) {
  var restArgs = Array.prototype.slice.call(arguments, 1);
  return this.each(function () {
    var instance = $.data(this, "plugin_" + pluginName);
    if (!instance) {
      instance = new Plugin( this, options );
      $.data(this, "plugin_" + pluginName, instance);
    } else if (typeof options === 'string' && // method name
      options[0] !== '_' && // protect private methods
      typeof instance[options] === 'function') {
      instance[options].apply(instance, restArgs);
    }
  });
};
```

In the above implementation, we used the first argument to identify the method that needs to be invoked and then invoked it with the rest arguments. We also added a check to prevent the invocation of methods that start with an underscore which, according to common conventions, are intended to be for internal or private use. As a result, in order to add an extra method to your plugin's public API, we just need to declare it in the `Plugin.prototype` that we saw earlier.

Another great way to implement your plugin when you are already using jQuery-UI in your application is to use the `$.widget()` method which is also known as jQuery-UI Widget Factory. Its implementation abstracts several parts of the boilerplate code that we saw in this chapter and helps create complex and robust plugins. For more information, you can read the documentation at: `http://api.jqueryui.com/jQuery.widget/`

Choosing a name

Lastly, after learning the best practices that we need to create a jQuery plugin, let's say something about the naming conventions and where to publish your new and shiny plugin.

As you have probably already seen, most jQuery plugins use the following naming convention: jQuery-myPluginName for their project sites and repositories and store their implementations in a file named `jquery.mypluginname.js`. After settling on some prospective names for your plugin, take a moment and search the web to verify that there is no one else with the same project name. The jQuery documentation suggests searching for plugins on NPM and refining your results by using the `jquery-plugin` keyword. This is obviously the best way to publish your plugin so that it can be easily found by others.

 For more information about NPM, you can visit: `https://www.npmjs.com/`

Another popular place for searching and hosting JavaScript libraries is GitHub. You can find its repository search page at `https://github.com/search?l=JavaScript`, where it filters the search results to include only JavaScript projects and searches for existing plugins and already used project names. Since in our case we are focusing on jQuery plugins, you will get better results by searching for project names that follow the aforementioned naming convention, jQuery-myPluginName.

 Until recently, developers could search for existing plugins and register a new one at the official jQuery Plugin Registry (`http://plugins.jquery.com/`). Unfortunately, it has been discontinued and now only allows searching for older plugins with no new submissions.

Summary

In this chapter we learned how jQuery can be extended by implementing and using plugins. We first saw an example of the simplest way that a jQuery plugin can be implemented and analyzed the characteristics that make a great plugin, and one which follows the principles of the jQuery library.

We were then introduced to the most common development patterns in the developer community for creating jQuery Plugins. We analyzed the implementation problems that each of them solves and the use cases that are a better match for them.

After completing this chapter, we are now able to abstract parts of our applications into reusable and extensible jQuery plugins that are structured using the development pattern that best matches each use case.

In the next chapter, we will present several optimization techniques that can be used to improve the performance of our jQuery applications, especially when they become large and complex. We will discuss simple practices such as using CDNs to load third-party libraries and continue with more advanced subjects such as lazy loading the modules of an implementation.

11
Optimization Patterns

This chapter presents several optimization techniques that can be used to improve the performance of jQuery applications, especially when they become large and complex.

We will start with simple practices like bundling and minifying our JavaScript files and discuss the benefits of using **CDNs** to load third-party libraries. We will then move on to analyze some simple patterns for writing efficient JavaScript code and learn how to write efficient CSS selectors in order to improve the page's rendering speed and DOM traversals using jQuery.

We will then study jQuery-specific practices such as the caching of jQuery Composite Collection Objects, how to minimize DOM manipulations, and have a reminder of the **Delegate Observer Pattern** as a good example of the **Flyweight Pattern**. Lastly, we will get an introduction to the advanced technique of **Lazy Loading** and have a demonstration of how to load the different modules of an implementation progressively, based on user actions.

By the end of this chapter, we will be able to apply the most common optimization patterns to our implementations and use this chapter as a checklist of best practices and performance tips before moving the application to a production environment.

In this chapter, we shall:

- Learn the benefits of bundling and minifying our JavaScript files
- Learn how to load third-party libraries through the CDN server
- Learn some simple JavaScript performance tips
- Learn how to optimize our jQuery code
- Introduce the Flyweight pattern and showcase some examples of it
- Learn how to lazyload parts of our application when required by a user action

Placing scripts near the end of the page

The first tip for making your page's initial rendering faster is to gather all the required JavaScript files and place their `<script>` tags near the end of the page, preferably just before the closing `</body>` tag. This change will have a great impact on the time needed for the initial rendering of the page, especially for users with low speed connections such as mobile users. If you are already using the `$(document).ready()` method for all initialization purposes that relate to the DOM, moving the `<script>` tags around should not affect the functionality of your implementation at all.

The main reason for this is that, even though browsers download the page's HTML and other resources (CSS, images, and so on) in parallel, when a `<script>` tag is encountered, the browser pauses everything else until it is downloaded and executed. In order to work around this limitation of the specification, attributes like `defer` and `async` from HTLM5 have been introduced as parts of the `<script>` tag specification but unfortunately have only started to be adopted by some browsers recently. As a result, this practice is still widely used to obtain good page loading speeds even on older browsers.

 For more information about the `<script>` tag you can visit: `https://developer.mozilla.org/en-US/docs/Web/HTML/Element/script`

Bundling and minifying resources

The first place to look when trying to make a page load faster is for ways to reduce the number and total size of HTTP requests. The benefits come from the fact that the browser downloads the content in larger chunks instead of spending time waiting for a lot of small round-trips to the server to complete. This is especially beneficial for users with low speed connections such as mobile users.

Resource concatenation is a simple concept that does not need any introduction. This can be done manually but it is preferable to automate this task with a bundling script or introduce a build step for your project. Depending on your development environment, there are different bundling solutions to choose from. If you are using **grunt** or **gulp** as part of your development stack, you can use solutions like `grunt-contrib-concat` (`https://github.com/gruntjs/grunt-contrib-concat`) and `gulp-concat` (`https://github.com/contra/gulp-concat`) respectively.

Minifying JavaScript files is a more complex procedure which includes a series of code transformations that are applied to the target source code, ranging from something as simple as white space removal to more complex tasks like variable renaming. Popular solutions for minifying JavaScript include:

- YUI Compressor available at `http://yui.github.io/yuicompressor/`

- Google's Closure Compiler available at `https://developers.google.com/closure/compiler/`

- UglifyJS available at `https://github.com/mishoo/UglifyJS2`

Once again, various solutions exist that integrate the above libraries nicely with your preferred development environment and make minification a simple task. Examples of integrations for grunt and gulp include `grunt-contrib-uglify` (`https://github.com/gruntjs/grunt-contrib-uglify`) and `gulp-uglify` (`https://github.com/terinjokes/gulp-uglify`) respectively.

As a final word, keep in mind that your code should be as readable and as logically structured as possible. Bundling and minifying your JavaScript and CSS files is most effectively done as a build step of your development and deployment procedures.

Using IIFE parameters

Apart from helping to avoid polluting the global namespace, using IIFEs to wrap your implementation can also be beneficial for the size of your minified JavaScript files. Let's take a look at the following code in which the `jQuery`, the `window`, and the `document` variables are passed as invocation parameters to the module's IIFE.

```
(function ( $, window, document, undefined ) {
    if (window.myModule === undefined) {
        window.myModule = {};
    }

    myModule.init = function() { /*...*/ };

    $(document).ready(myModule.init);

})( jQuery, window, document );
```

We saw a similar pattern in the previous chapter, as part of the suggested template for creating jQuery plugins. Even though the variable aliasing does not affect the functionality of the implementation, it allows the code minifiers to apply variable renaming in more places than before, resulting in code like the following:

```
(function(b, a, c, d) {
    a.myModule === d && (a.myModule = {});
    myModule.init = function() { /*...*/ };
    b(c).ready(myModule.init);
})(jQuery, window, document);
```

As you can see in the above code, all the invocation parameters of the IIFE were renamed by the minifier to single letter identifiers, which increases the gains of the minification especially if the original identifiers are used in several places.

> As an added benefit, aliasing also protects our modules from the case that the original variables get accidentally assigned a different value. For example, when IIFE parameters are not used, an assignment like `$ = {}` or `undefined = 7` from within a different module would break all the implementation.

Using CDNs

Instead of serving all of the JavaScript and CSS files of the third-party libraries from your web server, you should consider using a **Content Delivery Network (CDN)**. Using a CDN to serve the static files of the libraries that are used by your website can make it load faster since:

- CDNs have high speed connections and several caching levels.
- CDNs have many geographically distributed servers that can deliver the requested files faster since they are closer to the end user.
- CDNs help parallelize resource requests, since most browsers can only download up to four resources concurrently from any specific domain.

Moreover, if a user has static resources cached from a previous visit to another website that uses the same CDN, he or she will not have to download them again, reducing the time that your site needs to load.

Below is a list with the most widely used CDNs for JavaScript libraries which you can use in your implementations:

- `https://code.jquery.com/`
- `https://developers.google.com/speed/libraries/`
- `https://cdnjs.com/`
- `http://www.jsdelivr.com/`

Using JSDelivr API

A newcomer to the CDN world is JSDelivr, which is gaining popularity because of its unique features. Beyond simply serving existing static files, JSDelivr provides an API (`https://github.com/jsdelivr/api`) that allows us to create and use custom bundles with the resources that we need to load, helping us to minimize the HTTP requests that our site needs. Moreover, its API allows us to target libraries with different levels of specificity (major, minor, or bug fix releases) and even allows us to load only specific parts of a library.

As an example, take a look at the following URL, which allows us to load the most recent bug fix releases of jQuery v1.11.x with a single request as well as some parts of jQuery-UI v1.10.x and Bootstrap v3.3.x: `http://cdn.jsdelivr.net/g/jquery@1.11,jquery.ui@1.10(jquery.ui.core.min.js+jquery.ui.widget.min.js+jquery.ui.mouse.min.js+jquery.ui.sortable.min.js),bootstrap@3.3`

Optimizing common JavaScript code

In this section, we will analyze some performance tips that are not jQuery-specific and can be applied to most JavaScript implementations.

Writing better for loops

When iterating over the items of an array or an array-like collection with a `for` loop, a simple way to improve the performance of the iteration is to avoid accessing the `length` property on every loop. This can easily be done by storing the iteration `length` to a separate variable, declared just before the loop or even along with it, as shown below:

```
for (var i = 0, len = myArray.length; i < len; i++) {
    var item = myArray[i];
    /*...*/
}
```

Moreover, if we need to iterate over the items of an array that does not contain **falsy** values, we can use an even better pattern which is commonly applied for iterating over arrays that contain objects:

```
var objects = [{ }, { }, { }];
for (var i = 0, item; item = objects[i]; i++) {
    console.log(item);
}
```

In this case, instead of relying on the `length` property of the array, we exploit the fact that access to an out-of-bounds position of the array returns `undefined` which is falsy and stops the iteration. Another sample case that this trick can be used in is when iterating over **Node Lists** or jQuery Composite Collection Objects as shown below:

```
var anchors = $('a'); // or document.getElementsByTagName('a');
for (var i = 0, anchor; anchor = anchors[i]; i++) {
    console.log(anchor.href);
}
```

> For more information about the **truthy** and **falsy** JavaScript values, visit: https://developer.mozilla.org/en-US/docs/Glossary/Truthy and https://developer.mozilla.org/en-US/docs/Glossary/Falsy

Writing performant CSS selectors

Even though **Sizzle** (jQuery's selector engine) hides the complexity of DOM traversals based on complex CSS selectors, we should have an idea of how our selectors are performing. Understanding how CSS selectors are matched against the elements of the DOM helps us write more efficient selectors which perform better when used with jQuery.

The key characteristic of efficient CSS selectors is specificity. According to this, ID and Class selectors are always more efficient than selectors with many results like div and *. When writing complex CSS selectors, keep in mind that they are evaluated from the right to the left and that a selector gets rejected after recursively testing it against every parent element until the root of the DOM.

As a result, try to be as specific as possible with the rightmost selector in order to cut down the matched elements as quickly as possible during the execution of the selector.

```
// initially matches all the anchors of the page
// and then removes those that are not children of the container
$('.container a');

// performs better, since it matches fewer elements
// in the first step of the selector's evaluation
$('.container .mySpecialLinks');
```

The other performance tip is using the Child Selector ("parent > child") wherever applicable, in an effort to eliminate the recursion over all the hierarchy of the DOM tree. A great example where this can be applied is in cases where the target elements can be found at a specific descendant level of a common ancestor element:

```
// initially matches all the div's of the page, which is bad
$('.container div') ;

// a lot faster than the previous one,
// since it avoids the recursive class checks
// until reaching the root of the DOM tree
$('.container > div');

// best of all, but can't be used always
$('.container > .specialDivs');
```

The same tips can also be applied to CSS selectors that are used for styling pages. Even though browsers have been trying to optimize any given CSS selector, the tips described above can greatly reduce the time that is required to render a web page.

 For more information on jQuery CSS selector performance, you can visit: http://learn.jquery.com/performance/optimize-selectors/

Writing efficient jQuery code

Let's now proceed and analyze the most important jQuery-specific performance tips. For more information about the most up-to-date performance tips on jQuery, keep an eye on the relevant page for jQuery's Learning Center: http://learn.jquery.com/performance

Minimizing DOM traversals

Since jQuery made DOM traversals so simple, many web developers overused the $() function everywhere, even in subsequent lines of code, making their implementations slower by executing unnecessary code. One of the main reasons that the complexity of the operation is so often overlooked is the elegant and minimalistic syntax that jQuery uses. Despite the fact that JavaScript browser engines became many times faster in the last few years, with performance comparable to many compiled languages, the DOM API is still one of their slowest components and, as a result, developers have to minimize their interactions with it.

Caching jQuery objects

Storing the result of the $() function to a local variable and subsequently using it to operate on the retrieved elements is the simplest way of eliminating unnecessary executions of the same DOM traversals.

```
var $element = $('.boxHeader');
if ($element.css('position') === 'static') {
  $element.css({ position: 'relative' });
}
$element.height('40px');
$element.wrapInner('<b>');
```

In the previous chapters, we even suggested storing Composite Collection Objects of important page elements as properties of our modules and reusing them everywhere in our application:

```
dashboard.$container = null;
dashboard.init = function() {
    dashboard.$container = $('.dashboardContainer');
};
```

 Caching retrieved elements on modules is a very good practice when the elements are not going to be removed from the page. Keep in mind that, when dealing with elements with shorter lifespans, in order to avoid memory leaks, you have to either ensure that you clear all their references when they are removed from the page or have a fresh reference retrieved when required and cache it only inside your functions.

Scoping element traversals

Instead of writing complex CSS selectors for your traversals like:

```
$('.dashboardContainer .dashboardCategories');
```

You can instead have the same result in a more efficient way by using an already retried ancestor element to scope the DOM traversal. This way, you are not only using simpler CSS selectors that are faster to match against page elements, but you are also reducing the number of elements that have to be checked. Moreover, the resulting implementations have less code repetitions (are DRYer) and the CSS selectors used are simple and as a result more readable.

```
var $container = $('.dashboardContainer');
$container.find('.dashboardCategories');
```

Additionally, this practice works even better with module-wide cached elements like those we used in the previous chapters:

```
$boxContainer = dashboard.$container.find('.boxContainer');
```

Chaining jQuery methods

One of the characteristics of all jQuery APIs is that they are **Fluent** interface implementations that enable us to chain several method invocations on a single Composite Collection Object.

```
$('.boxContent').html('')
    .append('<a href="#">')
    .height('40px')
    .wrapInner('<b>');
```

As we discussed in previous chapters, chaining allows us to reduce the number of used variables and leads to more readable implementations with fewer code repetitions.

Don't overdo it

Keep in mind that jQuery also provides the `$.fn.end()` method (`http://api.jquery.com/end/`) as a way of moving back from a chained traversal.

```
$('.box')
    .filter(':even')
    .find('.boxHeader')
    .css('background-color', '#0F0')
    .end()
    .end() // undo the filter and find traversals
    .filter(':odd') // applied on  the initial .box results
    .find('.boxHeader')
    .css('background-color', '#F00');
```

Even though this is a handy method in many cases, you should avoid overusing it since it can damage the readability and performance of your code. In many cases, using cached element collections instead of `$.fn.end()` results in faster and more readable implementations.

Improving DOM manipulations

As we said earlier, the extensive use of the DOM API is one of the most common things that makes an application slower, especially when used to manipulate the state of the DOM tree. In this section, we will showcase some tips to improve performance when manipulating the DOM tree.

Creating DOM elements

The most efficient way to create DOM elements is to construct a HTML string and append it to the DOM tree using the `$.fn.html()` method. Additionally, since this is too limiting in some use cases, you can also use the `$.fn.append()` and `$.fn.prepend()` methods, which are slightly slower but may be a better match for your implementation. Ideally, if multiple elements need to be created, you should try to minimize the invocation of these methods by creating a HTML string that defines all the elements and then inserting it into the DOM tree, as shown below:

```
var finalHtml = '';
for (var i = 0, len = questions.length; i < len; i++) {
  var question = questions[i];
```

```
finalHtml += '<div><label><span>' + question.title + ':</span>' +
  '<input type="checkbox" name="' + question.name + '" />' +
'</label></div>';
}
$('form').html(finalHtml);
```

Another way to achieve the same result, is by using an array to store the HTML for each intermediate element and then join them right before the insertion to the DOM tree:

```
var parts = [];
for (var i = 0, len = questions.length; i < len; i++) {
  var question = questions[i];
  parts.push('<div><label><span>' + question.title + ':</span>' +
    '<input type="checkbox" name="' + question.name + '" />' +
  '</label></div>');
}
$('form').html(parts.join(''));
```

 This is a commonly used pattern since, until recently, it performed better than concatenating the intermediate results with "+=".

Styling and animating

Whenever possible, use CSS classes for your styling manipulations by utilizing the $.fn.addClass() and $.fn.removeClass() methods instead of manually manipulating the style of the elements with the $.fn.css() method. That's especially useful when you need to style a large number of elements since this is the main purpose of CSS classes and browsers have already spent years optimizing it.

 As an extra optimization step to minimize the number of manipulated elements, you can apply CSS classes on a single common ancestor element and use a descendant CSS selector to apply your styling, as demonstrated here: https://developer.mozilla.org/en-US/docs/Web/CSS/Descendant_selectors

When you still need to use the $.fn.css() method, for example, when your implementation needs to be imperative, use the invocation overload that accepts object parameters: http://api.jquery.com/css/#css-properties. In this way, the required method invocations are minimized when applying multiple styles on elements and your code is better organized.

Moreover, avoid mixing methods that manipulate the DOM with methods that read from the DOM since this will force a reflow of the page so that the browser can calculate the new positions of the page elements.

Instead of doing something like this:

```
$('h1').css('padding-left', '2%');
$('h1').css('padding-right', '2%');
$('h1').append('<b>!!</b>');
var h1OuterWidth = $('h1').outerWidth();

$('h1').css('margin-top', '5%');
$('body').prepend('<b>--!!--</b>');
var h1Offset = $('h1').offset();
```

Prefer grouping the non-conflicting manipulations together like this:

```
$('h1').css({
    'padding-left': '2%',
    'padding-right': '2%',
    'margin-top': '5%'
}).append('<b>!!</b>');
$('body').prepend('<b>--!!--</b>');

var h1OuterWidth = $('h1').outerWidth();
var h1Offset = $('h1').offset();
```

The browser can thus skip some re-renderings of the page, resulting in fewer pauses of the execution of your code.

 For more information about reflows, visit the following page:
https://developers.google.com/speed/articles/reflow

Lastly, note that all jQuery-generated animations in v1.x and v2.x are implemented using the `setTimeout()` function. This is going to change in v3.x of jQuery which plans to use the `requestAnimationFrame()` function, which is a better match for creating imperative animations. Until then, you can use the **jQuery-requestAnimationFrame** plugin (https://github.com/gnarf/jquery-requestAnimationFrame) which monkey-patches jQuery to use the `requestAnimationFrame()` function for its animations when it is available.

Manipulating detached elements

Another way to avoid unnecessary repaints of the page while manipulating DOM elements is to detach the element from the page and re-attach it after completing your manipulations. Working with a detached in-memory element is much faster and does not cause reflows on the page.

In order to achieve that, we use the $.fn.detach() method which, in contrast to $.fn.remove(), preserves all event handlers and jQuery data on the detached element.

```
var $h1 = $('#pageHeader');
var $h1Cont = $h1.parent();
$h1.detach();

$h1.css({
    'padding-left': '2%',
    'padding-right': '2%',
    'margin-top': '5%'
}).append('<b>!!</b>');

$h1Cont.append($h1);
```

Additionally, to be able to place the manipulated element back into its original position, we can create and insert a hidden placeholder element into the DOM. This empty and hidden element does not affect the rendering of the page and is removed after the original item is placed back into its original position.

```
var $h1PlaceHolder = $('<div style="display: none;"></div>');
var $h1 = $('#pageHeader');
$h1PlaceHolder.insertAfter($h1);

$h1.detach();

$h1.css({
    'padding-left': '2%',
    'padding-right': '2%',
    'margin-top': '5%'
}).append('<b>!!</b>');

$h1.insertAfter($h1PlaceHolder);
$h1PlaceHolder.remove();
$h1PlaceHolder = null;
```

For more information about the `$.fn.detach()` method, you can read the documentation at: `http://api.jquery.com/detach/`

Introducing the Flyweight Pattern

According to Computer Science, a Flyweight is an object that is used as a means of reducing the memory consumption of an implementation by providing functionality and/or data that are shared with other object instances. The **Prototypes** of JavaScript constructor functions can be characterized as Flyweights since every object instance can use all of the methods and properties that are defined in its prototype until it overwrites them. On the other hand, classical Flyweights are separate objects from the object family that they are used with and often hold the shared data and functionality in special data structures.

Using Delegate Observers

A great example of Flyweights in jQuery applications is Delegate Observers which, as we saw in the Dashboard example in *Chapter 2, The Observer Pattern*, can greatly reduce the memory demands of an implementation by working as a centralized event handler for a large group of elements. In this way, we can avoid the cost of setting up separate observers and event handlers for every element and use the browser's event bubbling mechanism to observe for them on a single common ancestor element and filter their origin.

```
$boxContainer.on('click', '.boxCloseButton', function() {
    var $button = $(this);
    dashboard.informationBox.close($button);
});
```

The actual Flyweight object is the event handler along with the callback that is attached to the ancestor element.

Using $.noop()

The jQuery library offers the `$.noop()` method which is actually an empty function that can be shared among implementations. Using empty functions as default callback values simplifies and improves the readability of an implementation by reducing the number of `if` statements. This is handy for jQuery plugins that already encapsulate complex functionality.

```
function doLater(callbackFn) {
    setTimeout(function() {
        if (callbackFn) {
            callbackFn();
        }
    }, 500);
}

// with $.noop()
function doLater(callbackFn) {
    callbackFn = callbackFn || $.noop();
    setTimeout(function() {
        callbackFn();
    }, 500);
}
```

In such situations, where the implementation requirements or the personal taste of the developer has led to using empty functions, the `$.noop()` method is useful as a way to lower memory consumption by sharing a single empty function instance among all the different parts of an implementation. An added benefit of using the `$.noop()` method for every part of an implementation is that we can also check whether a passed function reference is the empty function by simply checking `callbackFn === $.noop()`.

For more information, you can find the documentation at:
`http://api.jquery.com/jQuery.noop/`

Using the $.single plugin

Another simple example of the Flyweight pattern in jQuery applications is the
jQuery.single plugin as described by *James Padolsey* in his article, *76 bytes for faster
jQuery,* which tries to eliminate the creation of new jQuery objects whenever we
need to apply jQuery methods on a single page element. The implementation is quite
small and creates a single jQuery composite collection object that is returned on
every invocation of the jQuery.single() method, containing the page element
that was used as an argument.

```
jQuery.single = (function(){
    var collection = jQuery([1]);
    // Fill with 1 item, to make sure length === 1
    return function(element) {
        collection[0] = element; // Give collection the element:
        return collection; // Return the collection:
    };
}());
```

The jQuery.single plugin is useful when used in observers like $.fn.on() and
iterations with methods like $.each().

```
$boxContainer.on('click', '.boxCloseButton', function() {
    // var $button = $(this);
    var $button = $.single(this);
    // this is not creating any new object
    dashboard.informationBox.close($button);
});
```

The benefits of using the jQuery.single plugin come from the fact that we are
creating fewer objects and, as a result, the browser's Garbage Collector will also
have less work to do when freeing up the memory of short lived objects.

As a side note, keep in mind the side effects of having a single jQuery object returned
by every invocation of the $.single() method and the fact that the last invocation
argument will be stored until the next invocation of the method:

```
var buttons = document.getElementsByTagName('button');
var $btn0 = $.single(buttons[0]);
var $btn1 = $.single(buttons[1]);
$btn0 === $btn1 // this is true
```

Additionally, in case that you use something like $btn1.remove() then the element
will not be freed until the next invocation of the $.single() method which will
remove it from the plugin's internal collection object.

Another similar but more extensive plugin is the jQuery.fly plugin which can be invoked with arrays and jQuery objects as parameters.

 For more information about jQuery.single and jQuery.fly, you can visit the following URLs: http://james.padolsey.com/javascript/76-bytes-for-faster-jquery/ and https://github.com/matjaz/jquery.fly.

On the other hand, the jQuery implementation that handles the invocation of the $() method with a single page element is not complex at all and only creates a single simple object.

```
jQuery = function( selector, context ) {
  return new jQuery.fn.init( selector, context );
};
/*...*/ init = jQuery.fn.init = function( selector, context, root ) {
  /*... else */
  if ( selector.nodeType ) {
    this.context = this[ 0 ] = selector;
    this.length = 1;
    return this;
  } /* ... */
};
```

Moreover, the JavaScript engines of modern browsers have already become quite efficient when dealing with short-lived objects since such objects are commonly passed around an application as method invocation parameters.

Lazy Loading Modules

Finally, we will get an introduction to the advanced technique of Lazy Loading Modules. The key concept of this practice is that, during the page load, the browser will only download and execute those modules that are required for the initial rendering of the page while the rest of the application modules are requested after the page is fully loaded and is required to respond to a user action. RequireJS (http://requirejs.org/) is a popular JavaScript library that is used as a module loader but, for simple cases, we can achieve the same result with jQuery.

As an example of this, we will use it to lazy load the `informationBox` module of the Dashboard example that we saw in previous chapters, after the first click of the user on the Dashboard's `<button>`. We will abstract the implementation that is responsible for downloading and executing JavaScript files into a generic and reusable module named `moduleUtils`:

```javascript
(function() {
    'use strict';

    dashboard.moduleUtils = dashboard.moduleUtils || {};

    dashboard.moduleUtils.getModule = function(namespaceString) {
        var parts = namespaceString.split('.');
        var result = parts.reduce(function(crnt, next){
            return crnt && crnt[next];
        }, window);
        return result;
    };

    var ongoingModuleRequests = {};

    dashboard.moduleUtils.ensureLoaded = function(namespaceString) {
        var existingNamespace = this.getModule(namespaceString);
        if (existingNamespace) {
            return $.Deferred().resolve(existingNamespace);
        }

        if (ongoingModuleRequests[namespaceString]) {
            return ongoingModuleRequests[namespaceString];
        }

        var modulePromise =
            $.getScript(namespaceString.toLowerCase() + '.js')
            .always(function() {
                ongoingModuleRequests[namespaceString] = null;
            }).then(function() {
                return dashboard.moduleUtils
                  .getModule(namespaceString);
            });
        ongoingModuleRequests[namespaceString] = modulePromise;
        return modulePromise;
    };

})();
```

The `getModule()` method accepts the module's namespace as a string parameter and returns either the Module's **Singleton Object** itself or a falsy value if the module is not already loaded. This is done with the `Array.reduce()` method which is used to iterate over the different parts of the namespace string, using the dot (.) as a delimiter and evaluating each part on the previous object context, starting with `window`.

> For more information about the `Array.reduce()` method, you can visit: `https://developer.mozilla.org/en-US/docs/Web/JavaScript/Reference/Global_Objects/Array/Reduce`

`ensureLoaded()` is the primary method of the `moduleUtils` module and is responsible for retrieving and executing modules that are not already loaded. It first uses the `getModule()` method to check whether the requested module has already been loaded and, if so, returns its namespace object as a Resolved Promise.

The next step, if a module has not yet been loaded, is to check the `ongoingModuleRequests` object to verify whether the requested module is not already being downloaded. In order to do that, the `ongoingModuleRequests` object uses the module's namespace string as a property and stores the Promises of the AJAX requests that are used to retrieve the `.js` files from the server. If a Promise object is available then we can infer that the AJAX request is still ongoing and, instead of starting a new one, we return the existing Promise.

Finally, when none of the above returns a result, we use the lower case module file naming convention that we discussed in previous chapters and use jQuery's `$.getScript()` method to initiate an AJAX request to retrieve the requested module file. The Promise created for the AJAX request is assigned as to the appropriate property of the `ongoingModuleRequests` object and is then returned to the caller of the method. When, at a later point in time, the Promise is Fulfilled, we re-evaluate the module and return it as the final result of the returned Promise. Moreover, regardless of the result of the AJAX request, the Promise is also removed from the `ongoingModuleRequests` object in order to keep the implementation reusable in case of a network failure and also free up the memory that was allocated for the request.

> Keep in mind that the `$.getScript()` method might not work in some browsers when the page is loaded through the filesystem, but does work as intended when served using a web server like Apache, IIS or nginx. For more information about `$.getScript()`, you can visit: `http://api.jquery.com/jQuery.getScript/`

The only change that we introduced to the existing implementation of the `informationBox` module for this demonstration was to make it self-initializable in an attempt to reduce the complexity of the `ensureLoaded()` method.

```
(function() {
    'use strict';

    dashboard.informationBox = dashboard.informationBox || {};

    var $boxContainer = null;

    dashboard.informationBox.init = function() { /* … */ };

    $(document).ready(dashboard.informationBox.init);

    /*...*/
})();
```

Finally, we also had to change the implementation of the `categories` module so that it would use the `ensureLoaded()` method before using the `informationBox` module. As you can see below, we had to refactor the code handling the click event on the dashboard's `<button>` since the `ensureLoaded()` method returns a Promise as a result:

```
// in dashboard.categories.init
dashboard.$container.find('.dashboardCategories').on('click',
'button', function() {
    var $button = $(this);
    var itemName = $button.text();

    var p = dashboard.moduleUtils
      .ensureLoaded('dashboard.informationBox');

    p.then(function(){
        dashboard.informationBox.openNew(itemName);
    });
});
```

Summary

In this chapter, we learned several optimization techniques that can be used to improve the performance of jQuery applications, especially when they become large and complex.

We started with simple practices like bundling and minifying our JavaScript files and discussed the benefits of using CDNs to load third-party libraries. We then went on to analyze some simple patterns to writing efficient JavaScript code and learned how to write efficient CSS selectors to improve the page's rendering speed and DOM traversals using jQuery.

We continued with jQuery-specific practices such as caching of jQuery Composite Collection Objects, how to minimize DOM manipulations, and had a reminder of the Delegate Observer pattern, as a good example of the Flyweight Pattern. Lastly, we got an introduction to the advanced technique of Lazy Loading and saw a demonstration of how to load the various modules of an implementation progressively, based on user actions.

After completing this chapter, we are now able to apply the most common optimization patterns to our implementations and use this chapter as a checklist of best practices and performance tips before moving an application to a production environment.

Index

jQuery implementation
about 91
jQuery DOM Traversal API 92-95
property access and
manipulation API 95-97
jQuery.fn.on() method 26-29
jQuery Plugin
$.noConflict(), working with 179
about 176
characteristics 177
naming conventions 195
principles, following 176
wrapping, with IIFE 179-181
jQuery Plugin Boilerplate
methods, adding 193-195
URL 192
using 192, 193
jQuery principles
Composite Collection Objects,
working on 177, 178
following 176
further chaining 178
jQuery Promises
transforming to 146
jQuery-requestAnimationFrame plugin
reference 208
JSDelivr API
reference 201
using 201

L

lazy loading 197
Lazy Loading Modules 213-215
Level 2 Selector API 93

M

memory usage benefits
comparing 45, 46
Method Chaining 8
Mockjax jQuery Plugin library
reference 157
using 157

Mock Object Pattern
about 150, 151
actual service requirements,
defining 153, 154
Mock Service, implementing 154-156
Mock Service, using 157, 158
using, in jQuery applications 152, 153
Module Pattern
about 67
benefits 63
IIFE-contained module variant 75, 76
Immediately Invoked Function Expression
(IIFE) building block 67, 68
namespace parameter module
variant 72-74
simple IIFE Module Pattern 69, 70
using, in jQuery 71
modules
about 61, 62
acceptance 64
internal part implementation,
encapsulating 62
using, in jQuery applications 81, 82
modules, jQuery applications
categories module 83, 84
counter module 86, 87
dashboard module 82, 83
implementation, overview 87
informationBox module 84, 85
using 81, 82
Mustache
URL 165
Mutation Observer
URL 186

N

namespaced events
URL 60
namespace parameter module
variant 72-75
namespaces
about 61, 62
acceptance 64

Thank you for buying
jQuery Design Patterns

About Packt Publishing

Packt, pronounced 'packed', published its first book, *Mastering phpMyAdmin for Effective MySQL Management*, in April 2004, and subsequently continued to specialize in publishing highly focused books on specific technologies and solutions.

Our books and publications share the experiences of your fellow IT professionals in adapting and customizing today's systems, applications, and frameworks. Our solution-based books give you the knowledge and power to customize the software and technologies you're using to get the job done. Packt books are more specific and less general than the IT books you have seen in the past. Our unique business model allows us to bring you more focused information, giving you more of what you need to know, and less of what you don't.

Packt is a modern yet unique publishing company that focuses on producing quality, cutting-edge books for communities of developers, administrators, and newbies alike. For more information, please visit our website at www.packtpub.com.

About Packt Open Source

In 2010, Packt launched two new brands, Packt Open Source and Packt Enterprise, in order to continue its focus on specialization. This book is part of the Packt Open Source brand, home to books published on software built around open source licenses, and offering information to anybody from advanced developers to budding web designers. The Open Source brand also runs Packt's Open Source Royalty Scheme, by which Packt gives a royalty to each open source project about whose software a book is sold.

Writing for Packt

We welcome all inquiries from people who are interested in authoring. Book proposals should be sent to author@packtpub.com. If your book idea is still at an early stage and you would like to discuss it first before writing a formal book proposal, then please contact us; one of our commissioning editors will get in touch with you.

We're not just looking for published authors; if you have strong technical skills but no writing experience, our experienced editors can help you develop a writing career, or simply get some additional reward for your expertise.

jQuery UI
Development
Ben Fhala

jQuery UI Development [Video]

ISBN: 978-1-78216-296-4   Duration:02:06 hours

Tips and tricks to master the jQuery UI library and set up your own custom widgets and cool components

1.   Utilize jQuery UI to its full potential.

2.   Create your own interactions and widgets.

3.   Understand how to skin jQuery UI elements and themes quickly.

Mastering jQuery UI

Become an expert in creating real-world Rich Internet Applications
using the varied components of jQuery UI

Vijay Joshi

Mastering jQuery UI

ISBN: 978-1-78328-665-2   Paperback: 312 pages

Become an expert in creating real-world Rich Internet Applications using the varied components of jQuery UI

1.   Create useful mashups by plugging together different components along with APIs.

2.   Design your own widgets like captchas, a color picker, news reader, puzzles, and many others.

3.   Take your jQuery UI skills to next level by exploring the ins and outs and nuances of jQuery UI components.

Please check **www.PacktPub.com** for information on our titles

Mastering jQuery Mobile

ISBN: 978-1-78355-908-4   Paperback: 262 pages

Design and develop cutting-edge mobile web applications using jQuery Mobile to work across a number of platforms

1. Create spectacular mobile applications using jQuery Mobile to its fullest potential.

2. Build a complete and customizable professional, standard theme using advanced effects such as ChangePage, PageInit, and Swipe.

3. Take your web app to the next level by turning your native application with Apache Cordova.

Mastering jQuery

ISBN: 978-1-78398-546-3   Paperback: 400 pages

Elevate your development skills by leveraging every available ounce of jQuery

1. Create and decouple custom event types to efficiently use them and suit your users' needs.

2. Incorporate custom, optimized versions of the jQuery library into your pages to maximize the efficiency of your website.

3. Get the most out of jQuery by gaining exposure to real-world examples with tricks and tips to enhance your skills.

Made in the USA
Lexington, KY
30 August 2018